INIS BEAG
ISLE OF IRELAND

By JOHN C. MESSENGER

CASE STUDIES IN
CULTURAL ANTHROPOLOGY

GENERAL EDITORS
George and Louise Spindler
STANFORD UNIVERSITY

INIS BEAG

Isle of Ireland

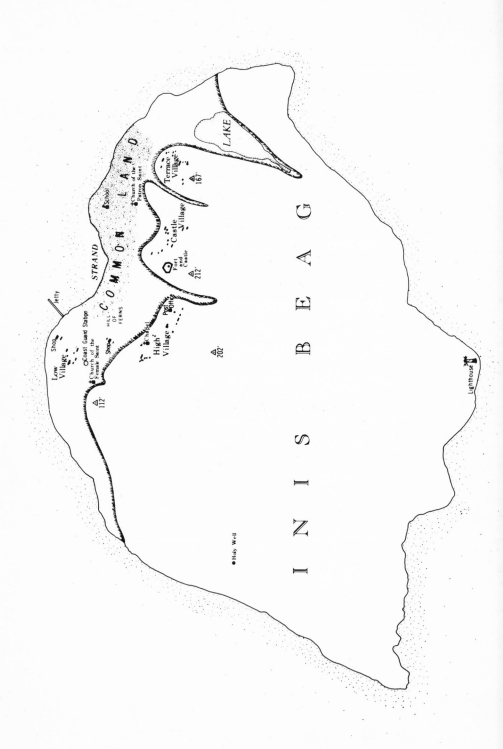

Low
Village

Jetty

STRAND

COMMON LAND

School

Church of the
Patron Saint

Terrace
Village

LAKE

△
167'

Castle
Village

Fort
and
Castle

△
212'

HILL
OF
FERNS

Coast Guard Station

Church of the
Female Saint

Shop

△
112'

Chapel

Shop

High
Village

Post
Office

△
202'

INIS BEAG

Holy Well

Lighthouse

INIS BEAG
Isle of Ireland

By
JOHN C. MESSENGER
Indiana University

HOLT, RINEHART AND WINSTON

NEW YORK   CHICAGO   SAN FRANCISCO   ATLANTA
DALLAS   MONTREAL   TORONTO   LONDON   SYDNEY

Foreword

About the Series

These case studies in cultural anthropology are designed to bring to students, in beginning and intermediate courses in the social sciences, insights into the richness and complexity of human life as it is lived in different ways and in different places. They are written by men and women who have lived in the societies they write about and who are professionally trained as observers and interpreters of human behavior. The authors are also teachers, and in writing their books they have kept the students who will read them foremost in their minds. It is our belief that when an understanding of ways of life very different from one's own is gained, abstractions and generalizations about social structure, cultural values, subsistence techniques, and the other universal categories of human social behavior become meaningful.

About the Author

John C. Messenger is a professor in the Department of Anthropology, the Folklore Institute, and the Program of African Studies at Indiana University. He received his Ph.D. from Northwestern University and taught at Michigan State University and Carleton College before joining the Indiana University faculty. In 1951 and 1952, he conducted fieldwork among the Anang of southeastern Nigeria as an Area Research Training Fellow of the Social Science Research Council; his research during 1959 and 1960, which provided the bulk of the data reported herein, was supported by an Exchange Scholarship to Eire administered by An Bord Scolairteachtai Comalairte of Dublin. Professor Messenger has published numerous articles, chapters in books, and monographs concerning the cultures of the Anang, the Irish, and the Montserrat islanders of the West Indies, whom he studied in 1965 and 1967. A grant from the Indiana University Ford International Program enabled him to write a substantial portion of this volume.

About the Book

This is a case study of a people widely known through the media of journalism and film. Imbedded in a context of romanticism and nativism, the image of the people and their culture created by these media scarcely approximates reality, for reasons that Dr. Messenger makes clear both in his discussion of nativism and the reasons for its strong influence on characterizations of Irish folk, and in his descriptive analysis of the culture and social structure of Inis Beag. For these reasons the book will doubtless raise controversy among Irish journalists, particularly those of nativistic persuasion.

Dr. Messenger describes the folk and their culture as he sees them, and within the conceptual structure of the social sciences. The picture that emerges is less heroic than the current romanticized idealization, and very human. The author's personal identification with the island and its people is obvious. He struggles to maintain an objective stance, and largely succeeds, but it is obvious that he and his wife participated exuberantly in the life of Inis Beag. This is in the best tradition of anthropological fieldwork. The problems of identification, friendship, rejection and acceptance, and ambivalence that are invariably associated with such participation are common to all of us who have had this kind of experience.

The case study is notable for its human qualities. It is a descriptive analysis of a significant folk way of life heretofore unrepresented in this series. It is also notable for its significance as an analysis of a closed community that provides mobility only by migration, and for the analysis of the influence of puritanism. This latter emphasis is particularly valuable, for too often we assume that puritanism is associated only with Protestantism. Here, the inter-relationships with Catholicism, particularly with the Jansenist denial of sexuality, is made very clear. Dr. Messenger pursues these themes at both the social and the psychological levels. The case study is also characterized by a strong focus, especially appropriate in the Irish folk context, on folklore, Christian reinterpretations of pagan elements, music, song, and dance. And the dimensions of life that are featured in most ethnographies are well developed—subsistence, material culture, social organization and social control, and values and religion. Dr. Messenger is also careful to provide a historical introduction to Inis Beag, in the context of relevant aspects of Irish history.

GEORGE AND LOUISE SPINDLER
General Editors

Portola Valley, Calif.
May 1969

Contents

Introduction

I NIS BEAG is a fictitious name for one of the many inhabited islands of the Irish Gaeltacht.[1] It is a rocky, barren protuberance in the ocean, buffeted constantly by wind and storm, where 350 hardy people eke out a meager existence. This tiny island is renowned not only for the distinctive folk culture possessed by its inhabitants, but for its numerous, well-preserved antiquities which attest to at least 5000 years of almost continuous human habitation, and its great beauty of land and seascape. During the past 150 years, first scientists, then writers, and more recently film, radio, and television producers have visited Inis Beag, and their many works have served to familiarize the world with the culture, albeit romanticized, of the islanders. As a result of literary publicity, which commenced in the first decade of this century, increasing numbers of tourists have been drawn to Inis Beag over the years. The cultural forms which are most publicized and attract the most attention from tourists are the traditional garb of the folk, their skill in rowing the famed canoe, called *curach*, the manner in which they manufacture soils and grow in them a variety of crops, and their Gaelic speech.

My wife and I were introduced to Inis Beag during a short visit to Ireland in 1955, when we viewed the island from the nearby coast and talked of its cultural past and present with scholars in Dublin, Cork, and Galway. Between 1955 and 1958, we immersed ourselves in writings pertaining to Irish history and culture, and during the three summer months of the latter year we visited several peasant communities on the mainland and three islands, including Inis Beag, of the Gaeltacht. We made plans to come back to Inis Beag as soon as possible to undertake research, and in 1959 and 1960 we were able to spend the greater part of a year there, during which time we visited briefly on three occasions a neighboring island—Inis Thiar[2]—and several institutions on the mainland to conduct library and other research. We returned eight times to Inis Beag and Dublin for

---

[1] The Gaeltacht—areas in which 25 to 100 percent of the inhabitants speak Irish—embraces portions of 12 northern, western, and southern counties and a population of approximately 600,000 people (Freeman 1960:166).

[2] In Gaelic, Inis Thiar (also a fictitious name) means Western Isle, and Inis Beag is translated Little Isle.

visits ranging in length from one to seven weeks between 1961 and 1966 to complete our project. During the 19 months that we dwelled on the island, most of our research was directed toward documenting the contemporary culture of Inis Beag: its technological, economic, political, social, religious, esthetic, and recreational aspects. We also investigated informal and formal education and the personality traits created by it, reconstructed Inis Beag history of the past century by examining historical materials of many sorts and probing the memories of elderly respondents, and recorded cultural change in process.

The research techniques that we employed are standard ethnographic ones: the guided and open-ended interview, external and participant observation, collection of life histories, photography, and phonography. Two departures from methodological orthodoxy were our use, as projective devices, of literary works and a sixty-two-verse ballad that I composed. A dozen islanders of both sexes and three age groups read at our request three books portraying Inis Beag culture, and we recorded and analyzed their varied responses. My ballad, now embedded in the island folklore tradition, is based on a shipwreck and rescue off Inis Beag that we witnessed, and a series of incidents which ensued during the following months. Alterations made by local singers after it was completed and the reactions to it by the islanders gave us insights into Inis Beag culture and personality which would have been difficult to obtain under other circumstances of fieldwork. I must add that the ballad was a product of exuberant cultural involvement and the satisfactions of "creative endeavor." Its research implications were unanticipated.

The Inis Beag islanders qualify as folk people in almost every respect, according to anthropological definition (Lewis 1960:1): the population has maintained its stability for at least two hundred years; there is a strong bond between the peasants and their land, and agriculture provides them with the major source of their livelihood; production is mainly for subsistence and is carried on with a simple technology, which includes as primary implements the digging stick, spade, and scythe; the island folk participate in a money economy, but barter still persists; a low standard of living prevails, and the birth rate is high; the family is of central importance, and marriage figures prominently as a provision of economic welfare; the island is integrated into the county and national governments and is subject to their laws; the people long have been exposed to urban influences, have borrowed cultural elements from other rural areas on the mainland, and have integrated them into a relatively stable system; and, finally, the experience of living under foreign rule for over three centuries has created in the islanders an attitude of dependence and, at the same time, one of hostility toward the government which continues to this day. The only conditions in Inis Beag which run counter to those in most other peasant groups are low death and illiteracy rates. The Irish shun the term peasant as applied to individuals or communities, for the same reason that elitists in developing countries eschew the term primitive as applied to traditional cultural forms found in societies incorporated into newly formed states. The causes of this attitude must be examined next.

During the past hundred years, Ireland has experienced a vigorous nativistic movement—provoked by seven centuries of English domination, linked with nationalism as the Irish sought to assert their independence, focused on the revival of a moribund language, and spearheaded by charismatic political, literary, and clerical figures.[3] A nativistic movement is a conscious, organized attempt by the members of a society to revive or perpetuate selected elements of its indigenous culture under conditions of acculturation with dominance. Such a movement provides the members of a society with psychological compensation for the frustrations engendered by cultural subordination; the revived forms come to symbolize the real or imagined freedom, unity, greatness, or happiness enjoyed by the people in precontact times, while the perpetuated elements become symbols of the society's existence as a unique entity, culturally distinct from the superordinate society. As the result of assimilating the values of the alien culture, a subjugated people will come to denigrate certain of their indigenous customs and will refuse to revive or perpetuate them, and sometimes they will exalt "racial" or personality traits assumed to be characteristic of their ancestors.

Although earlier influenced by Fenianism and the Gaelic Athletic Association, the nativistic movement in Ireland gained its full momentum with the formation of the Gaelic League in 1893 and shows few signs of waning today, more than four decades after the achievement of independence. The objectives of the league are to preserve the Irish language and extend its use as the vernacular, to further the study of medieval and modern Gaelic literature, and to encourage the cultivation of a contemporary literature in Irish. Spurred on by the formation of the association with its many local branches, Irish newspapers were established and Gaelic texts published which were read widely; Irish customs were revived, particularly in the esthetic and recreational aspects of culture; and Irish legends and history came to be "glorified."

> The language led inevitably to other things, to Irish music, Irish customs and traditions, Irish place-names, Irish territorial divisions, Irish history; it emphasised the separateness of Ireland as nothing else could; it brought with it national self-respect, a feeling of kinship with the past, the vision of a persistent and continuing tradition going back beyond human memory. The Gaelic League was not alone a re-discovery of the language but a re-discovery of the Nation, a resurrection of the Gael (an unidentified quotation from Inglis 1965:195–196).

Whereas the revivalistic emphasis of the nativistic movement has been on language and literature, the perpetuative emphasis has centered on religion. Since the fifth century, Ireland has been a predominantly Catholic country, and from the time of the Protestant Reformation religion gradually has become part of the warp and woof of the antagonism between the Irish and English. The basic differences in religion came to be fused with other national animosities, mainly political and economic in origin, and Catholicism emerged as one of the significant symbols of Irish uniqueness and superiority in the acculturation process.

It is readily apparent that the Irish have been extremely selective in their

---

[3] The next few pages and Chapter 1 will draw heavily on Irish history. I recommend to those readers not well acquainted with the Irish past two brief histories: Sean O'Faolain's *The Irish: A Character Study* and Brian Inglis' *The Story of Ireland*. The definitive longer works are Edmund Curtis' *A History of Ireland* and J. C. Beckett's *The Making of Modern Ireland 1603–1923*. The final chapter of the O'Faolain volume and Part III of the one by Inglis deal with Irish nativism.

choice of cultural elements to be revived and perpetuated. Countless forms of peasant culture, many of which are still widespread, have come to be demeaned and even their existence denied by the more militant nativists. The attitude of these persons toward traditional songs, dances, and sports such as hurling is quite at variance with that toward matchmaking in courtship and the belief in fairies, ghosts, and witches. It is the prevalence of such customs as the latter in rural Ireland which has been largely responsible for bringing the term peasant into such disrepute.

Some of the extreme points of view held by Irish nativists are: the Irish today are a "pure" Celtic "race" and possess psychological and behavioral traits which are "racially" rooted, including even a "racial memory;" Celtic civilization developed before and was "superior" to Greek and Roman civilizations, and the Irish branch of European civilization during the Middle Ages was "advanced" over those of other European societies; the Irish literary tradition has been "richer" and of greater esthetic "worth" than other European traditions of the past; the Irish language is a more effective communicator of ideas than other languages (especially English) and mirrors the distinctive Irish or Celtic "personality," "spirit," or "soul;" in order to achieve national identity, unity, and greatness, the Gaelic tongue once again must be spoken universally in the nation; and, Ireland is the "most Catholic" of all countries—in historical tradition, strength of belief, and morality. Inis Beag folk have been singled out for adulation by nativists because they are Gaelic speakers, pious Catholics, and believed to be lineal decendants of Celts who lived in the island two millennia ago. Their character is thought to embody those traits of ancient origin held in highest esteem by the Irish: spirituality, independence, self-reliance, industriousness, strength, courage, imaginativeness, sanity, and emotional stability.

Nativism has had a profound impact both on government policies affecting Inis Beag and other Gaeltacht communities, and on the interpretations of the Inis Beag milieu by writers and film, radio, and television producers. The extensive services and subsidies afforded the islanders reflect, in part, the nativistic outlook of the government; it is hoped that they will halt emigration and preserve the Irish tongue and other valued cultural forms which are preserved here but are disappearing rapidly from the rest of the country. Nativism also has caused artists, who have most observed and publicized the folk, to distort the Inis Beag way of life in their works. Too often they have been unaware of, ignored, exaggerated, or misinterpreted beliefs and behavior so as to present a desired picture of the folk, one in keeping with the nativistic stereotype.

Distortions of Inis Beag culture also have been caused by primitivism— the idealization of past or future cultural estates or of contemporary primitive and folk cultures. Like nativism, it provides psychological compensation for frustrations created by personal or social disorganization. Its origins are manifold and can be traced back to antiquity, but in its modern guise it is an amalgam of utopianism since the sixteenth century, Enlightenment views of "natural man," rural attitudes toward urban life since the industrial revolution, Marxian socialism, late nineteenth-century cultural evolutionism, and early twentieth-century ethnology. Central to the primitivistic position is the belief that civilization has dehumanized man and undermined his valued institutions; it has caused social bonds to disintegrate, fostered immorality, and created mental illness on a vast scale. Primitive and folk peoples, according to this view, represent man as he once was and could or should be again were civilized society drastically reformed.

Most of the ideas held by primitivists are as extreme as those maintained by nativists: primitive and folk societies possess simple, static cultures in which dysfunctional forms are rare; their economies are primarily subsistence ones, approximate the householding type, and lack competitive elements; social control is mostly informal; the family is the core social group and is a highly integrated and cooperative unit; religion is a pervasive force which sanctions most behavior and assures psychological security and social cohesion; and, religious dissent and skepticism are unknown. Primitivists also contend that primitive and folk peoples are content with their conditions of life, are seldom if ever mentally ill, and possess character traits that civilization has perverted. It is probable that primitivists would include all of the traits designated as Irish by nativists and would add many others.

The antiquarians George Petrie and John T. O'Flaherty during the 1820s were the first scientists to undertake research in Inis Beag and the surrounding region. Since that time, there have been short and sporadic visits to the island by a variety of investigators, among them anthropologists, folklorists, geographers, historians, philologists, and others. Most of the anthropological research has been conducted by archeologists, anthropometricians, and linguists. Several archeological expeditions have examined thoroughly surface sites in Inis Beag, but no prehistorian has excavated as yet, and the accurate dating of artifacts scarcely has begun. Reconstruction of a number of ancient monuments by the government was made possible through the research findings of archeologists, and today site descriptions on mounted plaques mark the principal monuments. Alfred C. Haddon and C. R. Browne in 1892 and E. A. Hooton and C. W. Dupertius between 1932 and 1934 made anthropometric studies, the latter as part of the Harvard University anthropological survey of Ireland, which also included archeological and ethnographic investigations. The ethnographic study—reported in Conrad M. Arensberg's *The Irish Countryman* and Arensberg's and Solon T. Kimball's *Family and Community in Ireland*—was made in three communities of Co. Clare by these authors with W. Lloyd Warner; it was the first holistic ethnographic study made in Ireland, and my research in Inis Beag in its initial stages was only the third. (The second, by Rosemary Harris, is reported in a 1954 M.A. thesis in the University of London—see References.)

Linguists, as well as philologists and those wishing to learn Gaelic, long have visited Inis Beag. There now remain only a few areas along the western seaboard of Europe where Gaelic dialects still are spoken, and the island is located in one of these.[4] One-half the population of Ireland spoke the vernacular at the end of the eighteenth century, but by the middle of the last century the ratio had fallen to one-quarter, or approximately 1,500,000 speakers. Sixty years later the

[4] The Celtic languages are Gaulish, Goidelic, and Brittanic, of which the first became extinct at the beginning of the medieval period, and the last two are represented today by the Irish and Scottish Gaelic dialects on the one hand, and the Breton and Welsh on the other. Two other related dialects are now extinct: Manx of the Isle of Man and Cornish, the British dialect of Cornwall (Dillon 1957:207).

number was reduced to only 580,000. The great famine of 1845 to 1852 and the tide of emigration which followed brought about a rapid decline in the use of the language. In addition, the elementary school system was directed toward substituting English for Irish, and until 1922 instruction in most schools was given in the English tongue. It was reported in 1946 that only about 40,000 persons in the Republic used Gaelic as their true vernacular (Freeman 1960:166–169).

All Inis Beag folk of the age of eight years and older speak English as well as Irish, many with greater fluency than mainland peasants, for English is taught in the school and is spoken with Gaelic in homes where a realistic attitude toward emigration prevails. As in most of Ireland before 1922, English was employed as the medium of instruction in the school, and sermons in the church were delivered in English; even today the islanders confess to their priests in English—a fact little known. The widespread ability of the folk to use English is not readily apparent, however, for several reasons: the people are subsidized by the government to have their children learn Irish at school, and curates have urged, even threatened, that the foreign tongue not be spoken on moral and nativistic grounds; teachers have ridiculed English speech idiosyncracies of certain students and adult islanders before their pupils and, as a result, have induced shyness among the youth; the secretiveness of many persons and suspicion of outsiders of others prevent them from revealing their linguistic aptitudes to strangers; a few folk are nativists themselves and shun the use of English for that reason; and, finally, I have witnessed islanders "cod" (jokingly misinform) outsiders as to the true language situation.

The English speech of the islanders, as is common throughout rural Ireland, represents a syncretism of Gaelic and English forms; that is, English vocabulary is merged with Irish grammar, and Gaelic phonemes and speech rhythms influence English pronunciation. Irish terms commonly are incorporated into English speech, and, conversely, English words form an important part of the vocabulary of the folk when they employ the vernacular. Nativists are extremely critical of English vocabularly borrowings, a point of view not shared by the islanders; the latter are equally critical of the creation of new Gaelic terms by nativists for cultural innovations. The folk, among themselves, also are critical of the language revival movement, since most of their number must emigrate to English speaking countries where lack of mastery of the tongue places them at a competitive disadvantage. Irish speech is judged by nativists as "good" or "bad" according to at least three criteria: the prevalence of despised English words, the retention of traditional Gaelic terms, and the richness of Irish idiom. Many observers, including linguists, believe that the "best" Gaelic in Ireland is spoken in Inis Beag and nearby islands; however, my wife and I had visitors from the mainland who were declared to be more proficient Irish speakers than the island folk themselves by Inis Beag people who met and talked with them. In this case, probing revealed that the evaluation was based on our friends' mastery of idiomatic expression and clarity of pronunciation. The ability of the native speaker to combine accent and idiom is known as *blas*, and the folk can ascertain readily whether a stranger has learned Gaelic "from the cradle" or "at the school" (called "Christian Brothers' Irish" after teachers of that order).

The most active researchers in Inis Beag have been folklorists. In 1846, 25 years before Edward Tylor pronounced his famous anthropological definition of culture, William J. Thoms introduced into English the word "folk-lore," which he defined as "the manners, customs, observances, superstitions, ballads, proverbs, etc., of the olden time." Ethnology, a scientific discipline whose focus is primitive culture in the Tylor tradition, has had for almost a century its parallel in the humanistic discipline of folklore, whose focus is the culture of the folk, or folk-lore, in the Thoms tradition. During this time, ethnology has evidenced a humanistic current in its concern with primitive religion, ideology, and esthetics. The discipline of folklore, on the other hand, has evidenced a scientific current, mainly in the research of scholars belonging to the "Finnish School," whose approach to cultural dynamics resembles that of the "American Historical School" of ethnology, and of eastern and northern European folklorists (who often call themselves ethnographers as well) who have been making rather broad cultural studies of peasant communities somewhat in the anthropological mold. American ethnologists employ the term folklore to designate only the oral literature of peoples— their myths, legends, folktales, anecdotes, proverbs, riddles, songs, and the like. I will employ the term in this sense when I deal with Inis Beag esthetics in Chapter 4.

Ethnology as a discipline is not represented in the universities and elsewhere in the Republic of Ireland, but folklore in the humanistic tradition is strongly developed (Delargy 1957; Dorson 1966). The deliberate recording of the immense body of folklore in Ireland began in the early part of the last century, was kindled by the Gaelic Revival, and was institutionalized in the Republic with the formation, first, of the Folklore of Ireland Society in 1926, then the Irish Folklore Institute in 1930, and finally, the Irish Folklore Commission in 1936. For many years, commission collectors have visited Inis Beag, recording mostly the oral literature and material traits, and their associated behavior, of the island folk. They have not attempted to describe and analyze functionally and dynamically the total culture of the people; moreover, their visits have been brief and intermittent, they have depended on a limited sample of respondents, and most of their queries have been guided by Sean O Suilleabhain's *A Handbook of Irish Folklore* (the Irish equivalent of the American *Outline of Cultural Materials* and British *Notes and Queries on Anthropology*), which does not include many categories of significance to anthropologists. Since my wife and I were interested primarily in the nonmaterial elements of Inis Beag culture, and since the oral literature of the folk has been well studied by commission and other folklorists, we placed less emphasis on material culture and folklore in our ethnographic work.

The culture of Inis Beag about to be described is that of 1959 and 1960, and if I intrude data from earlier or later fieldwork I will label them as such. My wife and I also collected a large body of cultural materials in three other Irish islands, for the purposes of making cross-cultural comparisons and testing hypotheses concerning culture and personality concomitants of island living. The Inis Beag tradition is shared in large measure by the inhabitants of neighboring islands, especially those of Inis Thiar, and the several cultures together might be regarded as forming a subculture of the Irish system considered as a whole. Many of the peasant customs of Inis Beag are shared with rural peoples on the mainland, where numerous regional subcultures exist, and some are part of a larger European matrix. In fact, as I indicated earlier, Inis Beag culture in its broadest outlines resembles other existing folk cultures. I have decided to employ English terms rather than their Gaelic counterparts whenever possible throughout the book, even though doing so will displease many Irish readers; this decision is based on the fact that most of its readers will be students of anthropology in colleges and universities in the United States. Since the islanders speak both English and Irish and command English equivalents for most Gaelic words and phrases, either language might be utilized.

The Island and Its Past

Prehistoric Period (9000 B.C. to 500 A.D.)

FORMED SINCE THE RETREAT over 12,000 years ago of the Weichsel glacier, Inis Beag consists of a block of limestone, Carboniferous in age, the geological axis of which is aligned northwest to southeast. The block has a gentle southwest dip, and its massive grey limestone strata are separated by narrow bands of water-bearing shales. There are two physical subdivisions in the island. On the northeast side, differential erosion has formed a series of terraces separated by small cliffs a dozen or so feet in height. The greater share of good arable land is found in this subdivision, where the shales have been broken down by weathering and alien soils deposited by wind and ice. These soils have been deepened artificially by the islanders through adding sand, seaweed, and compost. On the southwest side of Inis Beag is a more even surface, composed largely of pavement covered here and there by indigenous and manufactured soils, sloping from the 212-feet-high terrace crest almost as the dip of the strata to the Atlantic coast. The bare limestone surfaces are intersected in all directions by deep crevices, and in places the rocks form large slabs or are so fissured as to present a series of vertical ridges. Found in the joints are most of the natural flora—herbs and shrubs —of the island. The rocky appearance of the "back of the island" (see Fig. 1), as the people call this second subdivision, is accentuated by numerous granite and sandstone erratics dropped by the retreating glacier.

As yet no evidence of the Paleolithic has come to light in Ireland. The Mesolithic is dated from 6500 to 3000 B.C.; thus early man may have entered Ireland hard on the heels of the disappearing ice, as he did in other parts of Europe, crossing from the Continent on land bridges which then existed where the English Channel and Irish Sea now flow. A Neolithic period lasting only 1000 years existed in Ireland, and its artifacts at particular sites show a merging with earlier Mesolithic and later Copper-Bronze Age forms. Inis Beag contains a profusion of Copper-Bronze Age remnants, created before the coming of the Celts

Figure 1. The back of the island from the lighthouse

with an Iron Age culture about 350 B.C.; but only in 1961 were earlier Neolithic, or possibly Mesolithic, implements discovered. When my wife and I arrived in the island for a seven week visit during the summer of 1962, we were presented with three slate axe heads which had been unearthed by road workers the previous December. It is possible that they are Mesolithic, for the industry never has been dated accurately.

The principal Copper-Bronze Age monuments of Inis Beag are Megalithic tombs and burial mounds, and possibly kitchen middens and semi-subterranean stone dwellings, called *clochán*. Small gallery graves incorporated into lately built stone walls are common, but it appears that they never have been examined by prehistorians, for there is no record of them in the literature. Archeologists seldom have visited the back of the island where the prehistoric and medieval populations, contrary to present day opinion, may have centered. None of the Inis Beag *clochán* have been dated, but it is known that they were lived in by clerics and ascetics during the Middle Ages, and were still used as living quarters in a nearby island early last century. It is as difficult to ascertain the age of burial mounds and middens in Ireland as it is of stone houses, because they too were formed over several historical periods. Burial mounds of earth and stone, termed respectively tumuli and cairns by archeologists, first were erected during the Copper-Bronze Age and continued to be built into the early modern period (although not for funerary purposes). There are numerous mounds in Inis Beag, but in many instances it is hard to distinguish on sight cairns from *clochán* in their ruinous, overgrown condition. The islanders regard both types of structures as burial sites. Middens can be dated from the Mesolithic to the end of the medieval era. Most of the island middens are associated with dwelling places from the Middle Ages, but those located near the mouths of caves in the limestone cliffs of the terraces may be much older. I was told that foreign collectors long ago purchased from the folk copper and bronze artifacts which had been exhumed from cave middens.

The Iron Age in Inis Beag is best represented by a fort constructed of limestone rocks quarried locally and fitted together without mortar, which bears no name other than the Irish word for fort—*Dún* (see Fig. 2). It commands the rim of a promontory, and its oval shape measures 170 by 127 feet. Unfortunately, from the point of view of the prehistorian, its inner wall was greately reduced in height and any outer ramparts and stone *chevaux de frise* completely destroyed to furnish building materials for a medieval tower house which stands at its center. To the south about 500 feet, and on somewhat higher ground, are the remains of what may have been a monastery. According to island historians, it was pulled down by soldiers attacking the "castle" with cannons, and most of its stones were employed later in the construction of a watch tower nearby. Another monastery at the back of the island on the southeast side may indeed be the ruins of a fort, as the oldest of its three names bears the word fort.

Medieval Period (500 to 1500)

The end of the Iron Age in Ireland is dated conveniently by historians as 431 (or 462), when St. Patrick arrived from Wales as a missionary to convert the pagan Celts. But, of course, prehistoric cultural elements persisted for many cen-

Figure 2. Castle enclosed by the Iron Age promontory fort

turies afterward, and still do in modified form, and became embodied in the medieval culture which was shaped by internal innovation and borrowing from other European traditions. Christianity came to Inis Beag in the early decades of the sixth century. Inis Beag and the other islands in the vicinity became one of the famous monastic centers of Ireland, where over a hundred saints lived or paid extended visits. Among them were St. Enda of the Aran Islands, St. Columbkille who was to Christianize Scotland and much of England, St. Kieran the founder of Clonmacnoise, St. Brendan the Navigator who according to Irish legend reached the coast of Florida in 551, and St. Kevin the founder of Glendalough. Among the principal medieval Christian monuments in Inis Beag are three churches, one and possibly two monasteries, several tombs, and a sacred well.

Only a single female saint is associated with Inis Beag, and a church in her honor stands on the northwest side of the island. Although not the first church on the site, the present building was erected not later than the ninth century, and west of its doorway under a cliff is the foundation of a *clochán* in which the officiating clergyman may have resided. South of the church are a number of ancient tombs, and in a small valley east of it a layer of midden lies beneath manufactured soil. The axe heads were unearthed in the valley only a stone's throw from the church.

Built in the tenth century to honor the patron saint of the island, a second church is located atop a terrace overlooking the beach on the northeast side of Inis Beag. It was used as the regular place of worship until about 1840, when sand began to accumulate about it; at that time, the island cemetery was on a slight hill west of the church, but as the sand grew deeper burials were made next to the church, eventually to form the present cemetery which rings the building almost completely. The tomb of the patron saint stands on the surface of the terrace a short distance from the church, but it and the building nearly to the top of its gables are buried in the sand (see Fig. 3). Each year on June 14th island men dig out the interior of the church and bare the tomb to commemorate the saint. A huge midden, partially covered with sand and solidified to a conglomerate below its surface, is banked against the terrace on the north and measures 20 feet in depth, 150 feet in width, and 450 feet in length. It represents the accumulation of hundreds of years, and possibly thousands if pagan structures antedated Christian ones.

A third church lies buried beneath the sand close to the east end of the beach, and is named after another saint who is believed to be interred near it. Only legend supports its existence, for there is no reference to its unencumbered appearance in the writings of the earliest visitors in the mid-seventeenth century. However, funeral processions bound from the present church to the cemetery leave the main trail to follow what is apparently an archaic predecessor deep in the sand, and at one point the coffin is lowered and the mourners kneel and pray for the soul of the deceased at the place where tradition asserts that the ancient church lies. This custom is disconcerting to the newly appointed or visiting priest, who sometimes when leading a funeral procession will continue on the modern path while the islanders desert him to obey a centuries old prescription.

On the west side of Inis Beag, near the shore, are located a holy well named after a saint and the *clochán* in which he supposedly dwelled during a lengthy stay

Figure 3. Church of the patron saint and the cemetery

on the island during the early part of the sixth century. A low wall with two openings has been constructed about the spring, and it is visited frequently by those wishing to obtain water or to pray. I was told by the owners of surrounding fields that when they were children many gallery grave tombs stood in the area, but most of these were removed when the fields first were improved and seeded. Most islanders will not molest prehistoric and medieval monuments, especially those that they believe are burial places, out of reverence for the dead or fear of the ghosts or fairies who reside within them; but down the centuries, such structures gradually have disappeared by being torn down to satisfy building and farming needs. It is the emphatic claim of the folk that the sacred well was created miraculously by the visiting saint and has never dried up, but two unbiased observers reported to me that they had seen it waterless during especially dry summers.

At least twice during the Middle Ages Inis Beag was laid waste by invading forces: first by Vikings in 1081 (and maybe on other occasions between the ninth and eleventh centuries, when much of Ireland came under the control of Norwegians and Danes), and then in 1334 by Sir John Darcy, the Lord Justice of Ireland, who with a large fleet and army sailed around the Irish coast implementing British rule. The islanders believe that Inis Beag was completely depopulated by the Vikings and possibly by the Darcy expedition, and again by wars once, and maybe twice, during the sixteenth and seventeenth centuries.

Modern Period (1500 to 1900)

The castle in Inis Beag built within the Celtic promontory fort, probably erected in the sixteenth century by the mainland family who owned the island, is a three-story tower house with its south and west walls partially destroyed. The middle story of the castle rests on vaults, and there are carved corbels projecting from the north and east walls. It is believed that the castle was assaulted in 1652 from the land side by Cromwellian troops, who disembarked at the back of the island and hauled their heavy cannons across the limestone pavement, unimpeded by the stone fences which stand today, to the monastery above the tower.

Queen Elizabeth annexed Inis Beag for the Crown in 1586 because of its strategic position, after two contending Irish families had appealed to her following their fierce battle for its possession, in which all of the folk may have been slaughtered. From 1586 until the first decade of the eighteenth century, Commonwealth, Loyalist, and Williamite forces were stationed in Inis Beag most of the time, and until 1886, when obtained by the Irish Land Commission, the island was owned by a succession of absentee Anglo-Irish landlords. When Cromwellian troops forced the surrender of Loyalists in 1652, the population of Inis Beag once again may have been decimated, although one legend holds that only males were put to the sword. The island after 1655 became a port for transshipment of clerics who were exiled to the West Indies. This was the time when Cromwell revenged himself on Irish Catholics and their Protestant allies by appropriating for his followers more than half of the Irish soil and leveling harsh political, commercial, and religious penalties. Thousands of priests were banished, including all of the bishops for a time, in his crusade.

It was after the Restoration in 1660 that the land of Inis Beag was divided into quarters, half-quarters, and smaller units and assigned to families. My genealogical research reveals that all of the families of Inis Beag trace descent from immigrants who arrived in the island during and after the last half of the seventeenth century. The early arrivals, as well as any survivors, may have intermarried and interbred with soldiers posted in the island, for anthropometric and blood group analyses (buttressed by surname and historical evidence and local legend) show that the folk more closely resemble the northern English than they do their mainland cousins. A Dublin humor magazine featured a cartoon, not favored in nativistic quarters, showing Inis Beag men in traditional attire playing cricket.

The islanders still express considerable bitterness over the conditions of poverty and servitude experienced by their ancestors during the 300 years that they lived under alien landlords. All of the excesses of foreign domination suffered by mainland peasants were suffered by Inis Beag folk, but were aggravated by the ordinary hardships of island living. Little is known of local events in the eighteenth and early nineteenth centuries, until the island was "rediscovered" by Petrie and O'Flaherty. There was trading between Inis Beag and communities along the mainland coast for many miles, and ships passing by often dropped anchor at the island; but at that time this region of Ireland was very much isolated and seldom visited. A military garrison once again was established in Inis Beag for a brief period during the Napoleonic Wars, when the English feared an invasion of the British Isles from the west by French forces. A watch tower was constructed on the island, one of a chain along the Atlantic coast of Ireland, to give early warning of invasion.

The castle and watch tower still dominate the Inis Beag skyline, and the latter serves as a landmark for fishermen posting their nets. Another landmark, at the southeast tip of the island, is a 110-feet-high lighthouse built during the 1850s.

Written sources and local traditions disagree as to the effects of the great famine on Inis Beag. Some observers claim that the potato blight completely destroyed island crops, and the folk were forced to depend on secondary agricultural commodities, livestock, fish, and limpets in order to survive; conversely, others maintain that the blight did not penetrate the island until much later. According to my Inis Beag respondents, the blight did contaminate some gardens, but enough were spared so that the islanders were not greatly inconvenienced. In fact, potatoes were exported by some farmers to help feed starving mainlanders. Between 1841 and 1851, the population of Inis Beag increased by 62 persons, at a time when most other Irish communities had dwindling populations. The first record of substantial emigration from the island, mostly to the United States, was in 1822.

Contemporary Setting

Inis Beag has a northeast to southwest topographical axis, at right angles to its geological axis, and is a mile and three-quarters in length and a quarter of a mile less in width. A population of 350 persons inhabits four villages, and the island comprises 1440 acres. When giving directions informally, the folk refer to the beach side as the north side and the back of the island bordering the Atlantic as the south side; then, the sound separating Inis Beag from Inis Thiar becomes the west side, and the sound between Inis Beag and the mainland the east side. I will follow this practice when describing various geographical and other features in this chapter. Between the mainland and Inis Beag, a reef extending from the island far out into the east sound is a menace to shipping; it was on this reef within 200 yards of the shore that the freighter ran aground in 1960.

A large beach and a contiguous stretch of common land, which together make up over 200 of the island's 1440 acres, dominate the north side of Inis Beag. The beach is known as the "strand," following English usage, and lies west and north of the common land, about midway between the sounds (see Figs. 4, 9, and 10). It is thought that several hundred years ago arable land existed where the common land does today, and the strand was very narrow; but gradually sand accumulated, widening the beach and burying more and more farm land as it crept eastward. If one examines the Ordnance Survey Maps of 1841 and 1902, the slow encroachment of the sand can be noted. The common land was about half its present size in 1841, and 60 years later almost 70 acres of cultivable soil had been engulfed. The tops of fences projecting above the surface at the present time attest to the shifting of the sand, as does the buried church of the patron saint, and sand now threatens fertile plots on the east side of the island.

There are six major and several minor terraces in Inis Beag, of which the lower two underlie the strand, the common land, and two of the four villages. The lower terraces are broad and the upper ones narrow and precipitous, while weather-

Figure 4. Low Village and Inis Thiar from the castle

ing has obscured in most places the disconformities between strata. Four rift valleys indent the terraces, and the eastern one runs the entire length of the island to the ocean and holds a 90-feet-deep fresh water lake (see Fig. 7). This valley and two of the other three to the west of it running half the length of the island form two promontories on the upper terraces of which the other villages are situated. Indenting only the lower terraces, the fourth rift is a minor one; it forms the valley in which the axe heads were discovered. Wells are found in each of the rift valleys where shale strata are bared. The four villages, from west to east, are Low, High, Castle, and Terrace.

Located in Low Village (see Fig. 4) are two grocery stores, known as "shops," and an old coast guard station, and in High Village are the post office and church; other buildings of importance are the new school on the common land and the lighthouse at the back of the island. I already have described the monuments of historical significance so need not consider them further. The older of the two shops in Inis Beag is situated at the southwest margin of the common land, while the other stands close to the rocky shore at the north end of the community. Simply a large, narrow room on the ground floor of the two-story dwelling of its owner, each shop also serves as a public house, or "pub," where wines, spirits, beer, stout, soft drinks, and tobacco are sold. Benches along wall and counter serve the customers who linger, and purchases are made across the counter or in a small enclosed room near the door, called the "snug." The usual occupants of the shop are men who come to drink, smoke, visit with their neighbors, and sometimes purchase goods for their families. Women and children when buying provisions usually enter the snug for privacy and confer with the shopkeeper through an aperture opening on the counter. At night, the snug allows small groups of men to discuss matters of a private nature over drinks.

Coast guard personnel first were assigned to Inis Beag shortly after the lighthouse was built. Three guardsmen and their families lived in private dwellings in Terrace Village until the large station was erected after 1883 in Low Village, following which the contingent was enlarged to four men. The two-story structure contains four apartments, and these housed the families of the personnel until 1922. Now owned by the Irish Land Commission, two apartments are rented by islanders who sublet them to visitors; a third accommodates the nurse; and the other has been converted into a government sponsored knitting "factory" which employs local girls. One of the several outbuildings of the station contains the breeches buoy apparatus of the Coast Life Saving Service. The life saving company is composed of 15 Inis Beag men, hired and supervised by a branch of the Ministry of Industry and Commerce, and was responsible for the rescue of the freighter's crew in 1960—its only rescue operation since being formed almost 60 years ago. A boathouse was erected on the strand by the coast guard company, and now it serves as an all-purpose building: dance hall, trade school, storage house, and meeting place.

Health services are provided the folk by a nurse, a doctor who lives in a neighboring island, and medical and dental personnel from the mainland who visit the island occasionally for specific examination and treatment purposes. A much renowned mainland woman who lived in Inis Beag intermittently between 1903 and 1923 (and wrote a book about her experiences) was the first nurse to serve the islanders; but since 1932, the Lady Dudley Nursing Scheme of Dublin has maintained "Jubilee Nurses" in Inis Beag continuously, each one serving from one to five years. The nurse is responsible to the doctor, from whom she obtains medicines furnished by the county council, and handles most of the medical cases which arise. Bedridden patients and women who are secretive about their ailments are visited by her during two daily rounds, while after dark she is visited by other patients, mostly men, who are also secretive about their infirmities, and she may be called out on emergencies. The doctor comes to Inis Beag once a month and visits the seriously ill accompanied by the nurse, and in the case of emergencies at other times which cannot be taken care of by her, he is brought over in the lifeboat of the Coast Life Saving Service at her summons.

The post office in High Village is an adjunct to the house of its supervisor, just as the shops are to the homes of their proprietors. The office is a small room with a counter, separating the clerk and her desk and switchboard from those who do business there, and a telephone booth. A radio telephone serves the island and can be used between nine o'clock in the morning and six at night. A line runs to the house of "Number One" of the life saving company, which he alone can use in matters pertaining to the service during the prescribed hours. When the freighter ran aground before dawn, it was discovered by islanders who informed the company; Radio Eireann reported the plight of the vessel, on the basis of S.O.S. messages, in the seven o'clock news, but the company had reached the reef before the telephone was available.

Inis Beag has only a small church, known as the "chapel." After the church of the patron saint was abandoned, a house served as the place of worship for a time, then was superseded by the old chapel whose foundations can be discerned next to the new one. Built in 1899, the present chapel has a bell tower in its yard, and 500 feet from it on a trail leading north to the common land is a shrine made of cement depicting Christ crucified, which was constructed in 1950. A curate who lives in a rented house in Low Village looks after the spiritual needs of the people of Inis Beag and those living in Inis Thiar. He travels to and from the neighboring island by canoe, although occasionally he takes advantage of the ship servicing the islands when its schedule coincides with his own. The region has been served by a parish priest since late in the eighteenth century following the relaxation of the Penal Laws, but only in 1919 did a curate take up permanent residence in Inis Beag. Prior to that the island was visited by clerics from the parish church and sometimes from the mainland.

It is not known when the first elementary school was established in Inis Beag, but the islanders claim that at least some formal education was provided from the early nineteenth century on, first by landlords and then by the government. Today, a "national school" with seven grades, or "standards," built in 1943, stands on a terrace above the east end of the strand. Its 90 pupils are taught by three instructors, two of whom are local girls and the third, the "headmaster," an outsider. The base of the school building and the low walls surrounding it are banked with accumulating sand, which has created much resentment against the government for having put up the structure there rather than in a more protected location, as advised by the folk. The former school, located next to the watch tower on the promontory above Castle Village, was sold to an islander after it was abandoned, and he partially razed it to obtain valuable building materials.

Three keepers are maintained in Inis Beag by the Irish Lights Service. One or two men and their families made up the lighthouse personnel until 1929, when a severe storm greatly damaged the installation and caused the women and children to be ordered off the island for their safety. The keepers are rotated, with two men on duty while a third vacations for two weeks, and from time to time islanders serve as relief and maintenance workers and help unload supply ships. A symbiotic relationship exists between the folk and the keepers, wherein the former are employed in the above and other capacities by the service, and the latter dispense kerosene and other equipment, it is alleged, to pay for goods and services provided them, such as craft objects which are sold on the mainland for personal profit. The keepers attend church, utilize the shops, and occasionally pay visits to local households, and these visits are reciprocated by a few men and children.

Trails, wells, springs, land areas, and coastal features also figure prominently in the lives of the islanders. Place-names have been attached to each, most of which were created prior to this generation, although fields in certain land areas still are being named as they are manufactured. It is thought that many of the place-names refer to archaic events, persons, and geographical conditions, and legends have come to surround some of them. Others are meaningless in that their constituent words no longer are understood because of either sound shifts or sheer cultural loss. The derivation of place-names is a common topic of conversation, and often prolonged and heated arguments arise over, for instance, the identity of the man after whom a crag is named or the time at which buildings disappeared which give a trail its name. Folklorists have collected most of the place-names, and philologists have pondered the origins of no longer comprehended ones.

Trails also are referred to as roads or paths. Usually, they are bordered by stone fences from three to a dozen feet apart and are surfaced with fine gravel bound by clay. The 1842 Ordnance Survey Map shows that the network of trails in Inis Beag has remained much the same over the past century, although several new paths have been added and all have been widened or otherwise improved. In recent years, the government has subsidized road improvement for several weeks each year during December and January. A senior and junior ganger supervise a group of fellow islanders—composed of those owning the gravel and clay deposits utilized, those owning land along the right of way, and those most needful of unemployment assistance—daily until the money appropriated for that year gives out. Nine major roads lead from the four villages to the back of the island; they roughly parallel each other and are reasonably straight once they climb the terraces. Crossing the middle of Inis Beag from one sound to the other necessitates traversing numerous fields and climbing high fences, since the four short paths running east and west linking five of the main roads at the back are found near the Atlantic shore. On the north side of the island, a road connects Terrace and Low Villages across the common land. This is the only major east to west artery and is the most traveled of the ten trails; passing between the cemetery and school, fences do not enclose it, and often drifting sand covers portions of it and must be shoveled away. A series of short connected paths make it possible to travel east and west along the terraces from one village to another above the main road.

Water is obtained from four principal wells near the villages and from numerous, less dependable springs at the back and along the shores of Inis Beag. Most householders also capture rain water from eaves troughs in barrels or small cisterns. At one time, water was drawn from pools formed by the four major wells, but now it is pumped from government built reservoirs. These reservoirs occasionally are broken open and water obtained directly from them by islanders who believe that the sealed structures and pipes leading from them to the pumps foster contamination. The government also sponsors the construction of water tanks in fields to accumulate rain water for pastured stock. Three of the wells are located in rift valleys, and the fourth is near the chapel; a potential fifth one is in the valley south of the lake, but at too great a distance from Terrace Village to have been improved. Two minor unimproved springs used by villagers are situated on a terrace of the western promontory and below the post office. The springs near the coast and those at the back of the island are used mostly for watering stock, and they tend to become dry when rainfall is limited.

Inis Beag viewed from the top of the lighthouse presents a somber yet strangely moving panorama of grey limestone pavement and fences, with patches of green here and there. Many hundreds of fields meet the eye, about half of which support little or no soil, ranging in size from a fraction of an acre to over a dozen acres. Three decades ago, it was possible to move easily from east to west across the back of the island because the fences averaged only three feet in height; but since that time, government subsidies supporting fence and field building have caused most of them to be raised to heights of from five to ten feet. The folk are skillful fence makers, and many incorporate various designs into their handiwork by using stones of different sizes and shapes. Stiles or openings in the fences connect a few fields, but gates seldom are employed; a man simply breaks down a stretch of fence to allow a horse or a cow to enter a pasture, then quickly rebuilds the fence. The outsider who believes this to be an easy task usually ends up with surplus stones, a disfigured fence, and maybe bruised fingers when he attempts to emulate the custom.

The hundreds of fields are located in dozens of land areas which bear names. Most writers assert that each plot has its own name, but in reality numerous fields are located in any one area. Thus, a man might send his son to dig potatoes in Garden of the Cobbler, that is, in the plot that he owns there; another man might go to milk a cow in his pasture in Garden of the Cobbler. A field will be assigned a new name only if its owner has another one in the same area, and then he might instead call it, for instance, New Field in the Garden of the Cobbler. Some land areas bear the names of persons and animals, others refer to geographical phenomena, while a few are linked to long forgotten historical events.

Over 50 coastal features also are named, from the Harbor of the Churchyard on the north, to Point of the Periwinkles on the south. Most of the place-names refer to rocks, flags, points, reefs, clefts, coves, channels, pools, low cliffs, events of the past, and small strands which mostly have disappeared. The freighter ran aground on a stony reef named Strand of the Sheep. This was a source of wry amusement to the rescued crew, but at one time the beach provided safe footing for sheep driven there to be washed before shearing or sale. One of the best known features is Piper's Rock, which figures prominently in legend. It is named after an island musician who long ago entered a cave above Terrace Village, which supposedly travels under the west sound and connects with another in Inis Thiar, and who never emerged again. In later years, bagpipe music was heard issuing forth from beneath the sea off the rock now named after the luckless fellow.

Inis Beag has four landing places for small craft along its shores, but none are large enough to accommodate the 550-ton government operated "steamer," which visits the island two to four times weekly. The main pier, also called the jetty, is 300 feet long and 15 feet wide and is protected on its windward side by a wall five feet high. Located just west of the strand (see Fig. 9), it is the third structure to occupy the site; the first pier was built in 1878 and the second in 1913, and the present one is an enlargement of its predecessor. Smaller piers are situated east of the lake, to provide Terrace Village access to the sea, and near the lighthouse. The former is used mostly to unload peat, or "turf," imported by hooker from the mainland and to carry passengers to and from the steamer, and the latter only to transfer supplies from Irish Lights Service vessels which anchor in the east sound. A slip on the west sound near Low Village is used by crews rowing between Inis Beag and Inis Thiar in their canoes. When tourists come ashore in the island, they usually do so for the thrill of riding the *curach* and viewing the more accessible historical sites and the much publicized folk; they remain only the hour or two that the steamer is anchored off the strand. Inis Beag has had regular steamer service since 1891, and before that time small sailing boats plied irregularly between island and mainland.

Climate

Whether or not the steamer calls at Inis Beag, especially during the winter months when severe storms are frequent, is of considerable psychological significance. The importance of weather conditions as they impinge, both directly and indirectly, on this tiny island far out in the ocean cannot be overemphasized. Most activities, and not only farming and fishing, are more or less affected by the climate, and the past, present, and future states of the weather figure prominently in conversations among the folk. It is customary for individuals when meeting to talk first of the weather before turning to other matters, and some of the common greetings pertain to immediate conditions: "It is raining.", "It is windy.", or "It is a beautiful day." These are usually the phrases first mastered by non-Gaelic speakers who spend time in Inis Beag, along with the most used greeting—"God bless you." and its reply, "God and Mary bless you."

The year around climate of Inis Beag might be labeled cool, humid, rainy, and windy, at least by one living in the Great Lakes region of the United States. A perusal of lighthouse records for the decade 1951 to 1960 revealed a mean temperature of 42 degrees (all figures Fahrenheit) for the winter months, December to March, and 59 degrees for the summer ones, June to September. During that decade, the lowest and highest temperatures recorded in Inis Beag, both during 1955, were 28 and 80 degrees respectively. January was the coldest month, with a mean temperature of 39 degrees, and July was the warmest, with 61 degrees. The island is located in a climatic zone in which the average rainfall is 40 to 50 inches per year; the average number of rain days per year is 225, and the average June sun hours per day is five and a half.

> Westerly winds predominate in Ireland, though naturally a climate experiencing the passage of so many depressions has winds from every quarter at some time during the year ... Winds of gale force are most frequent in the northwest, where they average 40 per year ... Most of the gales are from a westerly direction: they are so severe a menace to shipping that many inhabitants of islands and remote coastal districts ... profit from periodic salvage hauls ... The absence of trees on the exposed western coasts of Ireland is usually regarded as a direct result of the exposure to westerly winds ... (Freeman 1960:50–51).

Snow usually falls several times during the winter, but it melts within hours as the temperature seldom fails to climb above freezing on any day. During the months from June to August, the sea and air are often warm enough to encourage "comfortable" swimming by tourists, usually off the strand. The islanders consider May the ideal month so far as climate is concerned, for the weather tends to be cool, dry, and windy; flowers grow in profusion and birds return in great numbers. March weather, which is much colder but also dry and windy, is called "hard."

All of the adults of Inis Beag are amateur weather forecasters; however, several old men are considered to be specialists in the art. Some households possess barometers, and forecasts on the radio are listened to attentively by those who own sets. But, in the main, the folk prefer to make their own prognostications based on traditional signs, most of which are sound meteorologically and the outgrowth of centuries of careful observations. I collected 250 of these signs and placed them in the following general categories: density, location, and time of mist; type of frost and heaviness of dew; size and position of rings around sun and moon; color and conformation of sky and clouds at particular times of the day; density and location of fog banks; position and time of rainbows; clarity, closeness, and color of Inis Thiar and the mainland; changes in the weather in relation to tides; actions of animals; and pains in the human body. Of special interest are the signs associated with animal behavior, such as the height at which swallows fly, the prevalence of fly hordes, the crowing of roosters and braying of asses, the position that cats assume at the hearth, and whether or not spiders weave their webs across trails. The expert forecaster will weigh together as many as ten signs before announcing his prediction, and I once collected 16 from an old man in Low Village assessing conditions 12 hours hence. Some signs are quite obviously undependable, among them the quacking of ducks which some say will "call" rain, and the scratching of floors and furniture by cats which, according to others, will point the direction of the wind following a shift in the near future. The folk believe that the moon and tides exert a profound influence on both weather and human behavior; my wife on one occasion was told that her "snappish" mood (the words of a neighbor, not mine) was caused by the new moon.

The climate, in part, determines the conception of seasons held by the islanders. Four seasons are recognized, but their duration deviates from the norm of Western culture. Winter is conceived as embracing only December and January, while spring is thought to commence in February and end in early April. The other two seasons are not so well defined, but most folk agree that summer takes up the greater part of the year—from April until mid-September—and autumn the remaining three months. December and January are regarded as the coldest months, during which time there is a lull in economic activities, but planting begins early in February. Although the prevailing winds during the year are from the west and southwest, for several weeks between January and mid-March icy winds blow steadily from the southeast quarter and cause much physical discomfort and illness. In late March and early April, temperatures rise rapidly, and some islanders believe that March "steals" three days from April so that summer cannot be expected until after April 3rd. The circumstances of the theft are revealed in a legend.

The reason that summer is thought to extend for so long is a psychological one: the folk dislike winter with its cold and dampness and attendant sickness and the sense of isolation from the world that it brings. Few outsiders visit Inis Beag during the winter, and often the steamer is unable to leave port or must turn back because of gales or high seas. It is not out of the ordinary for the island to be totally isolated for a week or ten days because of inclement conditions. From late January on, warm weather is anticipated eagerly, and I was told time and again that summer was imminent when spells of cold and rainy weather occurred between March and June of 1960. During a quarrel with her husband over his confident weather forecasting ability, a woman noted for being an outspoken realist declared, "Inis Beag has only one summer month—July."

The island experiences but eight hours of daylight, from nine o'clock in the morning until five in the afternoon, at the time of the winter solstice, and only four hours of relative darkness, from midnight on, six months later at midsummer. People tend to sleep late during the winter, sometimes to nine or even ten o'clock, and to begin their social activities early in the evening, while in June and July they arise an hour or two earlier and work as late as ten o'clock at night. My wife and I have attended parties during the 12 days of Christmas when guests assembled before eight o'clock, whereas in July we have waited until almost midnight for festivities to commence, when darkness afforded privacy of movement, desirable for reasons to be explained later. Times for meals, feeding and milking cattle, and many other enterprises also follow the lengthening and shortening of daylight hours from season to season.

2

The Land and the Sea

Standard of Living

THE STANDARD OF LIVING of the folk has improved vastly since the establishment of the Irish Land Commission in 1881 and the Congested Districts Board ten years later, and the islanders are better off today than the inhabitants of some other areas of the Gaeltacht. In 1891, the Congested Districts were delineated as regions in which the population did not possess sufficient land to maintain life except at an extremely low standard. Between that year and 1951, the population in the districts declined 42 percent—from 541,000 to 367,000 persons. The few areas which would rank as congested now, on the 1891 basis, are mainly in Cos. Donegal, Mayo, and Galway (Freeman 1960:121–123). A vigorous and continuing effort to stem the tide of emigration, in part caused by poverty, led the commission, the board, subsequently the Gaeltacht Eireann which replaced the board after 1925, and other government agencies appointed in this century, to improve the standard of living by various actions: the enlargement of land holdings for more effective farming, the encouragement of small factory and domestic industries, the improvement of fishing, the construction of public works, and the introduction of various subsidies. Seasonal laboring in England, often practiced out of necessity by mainland farmers but not by the islanders, and remittances from relatives who have emigrated are income sources which also have served to alleviate poverty; but the major palliative throughout Ireland has been emigration. One of the factors limiting migration from Inis Beag to the mainland until recent decades was the low standard of living which prevailed in the country at large. An islander could not escape local hardships and privations by emigrating to urban centers as he can today; he had to turn his back on Ireland.

Most Inis Beag people believe themselves to be materially poor, although they resent others agreeing publicly with this view. A well-known Dublin newspaper feature writer in 1963 was denounced, and a vow made not to permit him to come ashore in the future, for his use of the term poverty when describing Inis Beag life in a series of articles. The islanders, however, constantly complain of their indigence privately and deprecate it and are embarrassed by it in the presence of strangers. Girls and young women are particularly disparaging, and elders are puzzled by this attitude because the lot of youth is so much easier than was that of their mothers and grandmothers. Those persons who extol island existence usually do so in a defensive manner; after conceding that goods are in short supply, albeit "no one suffers from want of food or clothing," they go on to stress the healthy climate of the island, the freedom and independence that they enjoy, the sanctity of Inis Beag and its many saints of the past, and the strength of Catholic belief. Sometimes the advocate is followed by a denunciation of urban life, where these essential characteristics are lacking, or by a recounting of the difficulties being encountered by a relative just arrived in Boston or London.

The subsistence economy of Inis Beag always has been dominated by agricultural pursuits, contrary to frequent assertions by writers that farming was subsidiary to fishing two generations ago. Most householders own land on which they grow potatoes and other vegetables, grass, and sometimes sally rods, and where they pasture cattle, sheep, goats, horses, and asses. Potatoes are the staple crop, and after they are harvested the land usually is seeded with grass and used as pasturage for a number of years before being replanted. Indigenous soils bearing grass at the back of the island also serve as pasturage, and horses and asses at times are permitted to roam the trails and common land to forage whatever they can from the meager flora there. Supplementing potatoes in the diet are various vegetables, milk from cows and nanny goats, meat from island sheep and poultry, fish, and other foods, many of which are imported and sold in the shops. Rye is grown for thatching houses and contiguous outbuildings, as well as barns located south of the terrace crest, and sally rods are used to weave several types of containers. The only vehicles in Inis Beag are three two-wheeled carts employed to transport heavy loads, such as building stones, along the rough and narrow trails. Most householders own asses or horses, often ridden, which carry burdens in baskets or pull carts. Other subsistence activities are knitting, weaving, crocheting, tailoring, shoemaking, and net making, although the last skill almost has died out.

A slowly expanding cash economy features the export of cattle and sheep reared or fattened in the island and of surplus potatoes, the collection of seaweed for extraction of its iodine content at a mainland factory, the manufacture of craft objects, and the keeping of tourists in private homes. Among the craft commodities produced are cable-knit sweaters, miniature *curach*, stockings knitted at the local factory in the coast guard station, and articles of clothing worn by the folk—woven belts, cowhide shoes, and shawls. These goods are sold both to visitors and to middlemen who resell them in Ireland and export them abroad. The cash economy is buttressed considerably by government subsidies of many sorts and by remittances from emigrant kin. Not only are income and property taxes not collected in Inis Beag, but rents are extremely low, both of which conditions represent indirect government subsidization. Income information is as difficult to come by as data concerning pagan supernatural beliefs, disputes, and sexual attitudes and practices; for the islanders do not wish to jeopardize unemployment assistance and old age benefits, nor to be taxed in the future, and thus closely guard sources and amounts of income, even from relatives and friends.

Division of Labor

The division of labor between the sexes is more dichotomous today than it was at the turn of the century, when there was an extensive sharing of the same tasks by men and women. The latter now restrict their economic activities to the home, for the most part, especially if they must care for infants and young children. As soon as children can speak and walk, they help their mothers perform household chores and run errands, such as carrying messages and procuring groceries in the shops. But at age seven, following First Communion, boys spend less time with their mothers and come to take on small jobs which throw them more and more into contact with their older brothers, their fathers, and other men of the island. By the time young adolescents pass Confirmation and leave school, at the time of puberty, they are able to perform most adult economic tasks, and their labor is of utmost importance to the family.

Among the major jobs performed by women outside of the household round, and these by only a few younger women, are cleaning fish, carrying seaweed, planting potatoes, haying, growing vegetables, feeding and milking cattle, and caring for poultry. They also knit, crochet, ready wool for weaving, and tailor clothes for themselves and their families, as well as make sweaters, belts, and shawls for sale. In the several homes which accommodate tourists during the summer months, most of the responsibilities for their care fall on the women of the household. Men also do the tasks associated with fishing, farming, and the care of large livestock just listed, and they participate in the job of thickening wool; all of the other subsistence and income activities are exclusively male ones.

In the past, when fishing was a more practiced and laborious occupation than it is now, women not only aided men gut and cure fish, but they baited lines and did other affiliated chores as well. They also participated to a greater degree than today in collecting seaweed and in planting, cultivating, and harvesting crops of all varieties. Their involvement in the economic life of the island often demanded that they transport heavy loads manually for long distances, especially when they cared for all of the needs of both large and small livestock and aided in kelp-making. It is not difficult to comprehend why women are mystified at the complaints of their single daughters about the hardships that young married women must endure.

Most folk admit that members of the present generation work less strenuously than did those of two generations ago, when harsh landlords rather than a benevolent government intruded so importantly into their lives. There is in Inis Beag a widespread feeling of guilt among men, seldom expressed openly, about being "lazy." It is my observation that island men, on the whole, put in fewer hours of labor and expend less energy than workers in a typical industrial plant in America. Inis Beag emigrants who return from England for visits invariably complain about how difficult their new work regime is when compared to the old. Young men are chided by their elders, as well as by their wives, about how much less they labor today than did their forerunners and womenfolk. One of the most popular conversational themes among old men is the contrast between generations—how much stronger and more industrious those of the "hero breed" (a term favored by Mullen [1936] in describing Irish islanders of the past) living half a century ago were than men are nowadays. Women are provoked by how vociferously their spouses complain of the difficulty and endlessness of their labor, and yet how little initiative and industry they exhibit and how often they are idle. "Light work" or no work at all is customary on days when the steamer calls, when it rains heavily, on the day an islander dies and two days afterward, on Sundays and holydays of obligation, and at other times, contrary to the state of affairs which prevailed in the past.

Several men admitted to me their guilt about not working more often and energetically, and told me that many of their fellows "talk big" but do not match their words with deeds. All of them questioned the need for maintaining traditional patterns of labor in light of the many supports to the economy provided by the government. One candid islander suggested that a factory be constructed in Inis Beag which would employ all of the men two to four hours each morning— "Then people would have a steady income and a lot of time off. Now it is hard to get up in the morning and decide what to do, and by noon you are just reaching a decision." An even franker man, of the oldest generation, was unwilling to agree with his peers about how hard they had worked when young. He was willing to acknowledge that now "times are easier," but that when he was a youth men often were idle and were chided by their elders and felt guilty. Interestingly, he was aware of the phenomenon of primitivism, which he described as "the romantic notions writers have about us."

Land Ownership

Inis Beag comprises a townland of four 256-acre quarters, called "carrows." Other land units are the half-quarter, the "cartron" of 64 acres, the half-cartron, the fourth or "croggery" of 16 acres, the half-croggery, the acre, and the three-quarter, half-, and quarter-acre. I have mentioned already that the total acreage of the island is 1440, the strand and common land together make up 200 acres, and the initial division of land among the local inhabitants probably was accomplished by a landlord late in the seventeenth century. Approximately 1000 acres are owned by the Irish Land Commission today and rented to 57 landholders, while two other properties have been purchased from the commission and thus are owned privately. The acreage not accounted for represents shore areas which are useless for agricultural and grazing purposes. Rent is charged according to the fourth and is 5 shillings[1] per year at the present time.

The quarters of Inis Beag extend southward in roughly parallel fashion from the four villages, and each landholder possesses numerous fields, ranging in

---

[1] A shilling is the equivalent of 14 cents and a pound $2.80 in United States currency.

size from fourths to quarter-acres, located along the quarter that his community fronts. As a result of past inheritance and purchase, however, five Castle villagers own plots in one or two other quarters, as do five High and two Low villagers. Before field building commenced, the most extensive and fertile soils were found on the terraces; shallow and less widespread soils were situated just south of the terrace crest, while the back of the island was, and still is, mostly limestone pavement. Landholders originally were assigned equal acreage in each of these three areas, so that no one would have an advantage over his neighbors, and this pattern still predominates. The quarters are separated from one another by high, thick stone fences which run almost the length of Inis Beag, and, from west to east, they are known as Quarter of the *Phoillín* (derivation unknown), Quarter of the Ridge of Huts (after an ancient *clochán* settlement behind High Village), Quarter of the Castle, and Quarter of the Lake; they embrace, respectively, 271, 261, 240, and 263 acres.

Fifty-nine of the 71 householders in Inis Beag hold or own land, and one of these is an absentee holder. If an individual possesses four or fewer acres, he is regarded as landless—"a man of few gardens"—and 11 men are so designated. Two as yet unresolved disputes over the possession of land when resolved will add two other householders to the landless category, unless the property is divided in some manner among all four litigants by the Irish Land Commission. The folk prefer to rent rather than to own land, so that the commission will supervise matters relating to inheritance "fairly" and with little cost to the litigants should a dispute arise. The average sized Inis Beag holding is 15.7 acres, or approximately a croggery, and 25 islanders hold this amount of land; in addition, one person has 40 acres, three 32 acres, one 28 acres, eight 24 acres, eight 20 acres, four 12 acres, and nine 8 acres. Below is a chart summing up ownership data by village:

	Landholders and Owners	Landless Householders	Average Sized Holding (in acres)
Low Village	17	9	11.0
High Village	14	1	18.2
Castle Village	15	2	19.0
Terrace Village	13	1	16.4

The disproportionate number of landless persons in Low are, for the most part, either descendants of fisherfolk who centered in that community in earlier times and did not possess land, or siblings of landholders who chose not to emigrate. They support themselves by craft work, keeping tourists, fishing, managing shops, and working for the government, among other pursuits.

Farming

There is neither legendary nor historical evidence of when soil building commenced in Inis Beag, but the process is an archaic one and is practiced in other communities along the Atlantic seaboard where appropriate seaweeds are available. Today, between 45 and 50 percent of the land surface of the island is soil covered. There was little "field-making" at the beginning of this century, and few plots south of the terrace crest were utilized for farming. Fields on the terraces were planted yearly with potatoes and other vegetables, but in the 1920s the "eelworm" parasite invaded the island and forced the present custom of fallowing plots for at least four years. This development necessitated the creation of new fields at the back, and when the government began to subsidize field making during the 1930s, and fence construction later on, another impetus to the manufacture of additional land was provided. Most of the literature pertaining to Inis Beag, influenced by nativism and primitivism, claims that field and fence building has proceeded for centuries (even millennia) and disavows the existence of indigenous soils.

The year in Inis Beag commences in February with the advent of spring, when seaweed is gathered, fields are manufactured, and crops are planted. Although some seaweed is collected in the summer and autumn and stored in "cocks" near the shore or in outbuildings for later use, most of it is cut and pulled in January and February at the time of spring tides. There is a maximum 15¾ feet difference between flood and ebb spring tides in Inis Beag, and normally submerged reefs rich in seaweed are bared three to four hours daily for two or three days twice each month. The men await a "good strand" to gather seaweed, when the tide is lowest during the daylight hours and not influenced by wave or swell action, for this is a dangerous task which sometimes demands wading in water thigh deep. The folk are amused greatly by a sequence from a noted film about them depicting a woman carrying seaweed along the coast during a raging storm; the footage was created by the producer to satisfy esthetic canons and to portray the primitive and Celtic virtues.

The generic term for natural fertilizers is "manure" and includes seaweed, compost, and guano. The islanders also use chemical fertilizers to some extent, particularly in areas where soils are deficient in manganese. Compost varies much in composition and may include human and animal feces, called "dung," turf ashes, and decaying vegetable matter, such as ferns and the sod "scraws" of thatched roofs being dismantled. Nowhere in the literature is the use of human manure mentioned, and the folk are extremely secretive about its use, as they also are about burning cow dung for fuel in times of emergency. Their reticence about disclosing these practices is a product of sexual puritanism. Young farmers are more willing than their elders to follow the advice of the Department of Agriculture agent stationed in a neighboring island, and are coming to use chemical fertilizers more commonly than was the case in the past. The islanders eschew artificial commodities which impinge on the human body, and often I have heard chemical fertilizers denounced because they supposedly are manufactured from "bones of evil persons buried in cemeteries" on the Continent, or victims of the plague centuries ago. Some farmers hold artificial fertilizers to blame for both the potato blight and the eelworm parasite.

Four kinds of seaweed are utilized by the folk: ribbon weed, string weed or sea thong, red or May weed, and black weed or bladder wrack. The most commonly used variety is red weed, once the major source of kelp, which is washed in the year around and is stripped of its leaves when collected. Its stems are known as "sea rods" and are accumulated by several islanders, dried, and shipped by small boat in May or June to a factory on the mainland to be processed for their iodine content. One man received 90 pounds for his sea rods in the spring of 1960. Ribbon and black weed usually are cut at the time of planting and are carried immediately to the fields, while the other two types are pulled throughout the year and stacked along the coast or in outbuildings. The most effective seaweed fertilizer is black weed, because its "sap" permeates the soil most rapidly; but it and string weed are in short supply in Inis Beag and are most available to Terrace villagers.

Any landowner can collect seaweed on the strand and along the shore bordering the western part of the common land. So much red weed washed ashore on the easily accessible beach during December of 1959 that men from all four villages gathered it during the Christmas season, when work usually is at a stand-still. Along the rest of the Inis Beag coast, areas for seaweed collecting are assigned to each village and to every family holding land within the community. Low Village gathers along the west sound, although a short strip of shoreline is assigned to High; Castle and High have collection rights along the eastern portion of the common land, and they also gather from the Atlantic coast near the ends of the roads leading from their respective communities; and, Terrace obtains its seaweed along the east sound, except for areas near the lighthouse assigned to Castle families. Long ago, a portion of the Quarter of the Castle was assigned to the Quarter of the Lake, but the traditional seaweed rights near the lighthouse were maintained.

On days suited for seaweed collecting, the coastline of Inis Beag is alive with moving forms during the several hours that the tide has ebbed. Men wade out on the bared reefs to cut or pull plants, which they pile in woven sally rod baskets, called "creels," and carry to horses and asses tethered on the paths above "high water mark." Sometimes a man will lead his ass to the edge of the water and load it directly, if footing is secure, and he may be aided in the task of carrying creels by his wife and children. The weed then is transported to the fields and dried on the fences or placed directly on the "gardens;" weed which has been stored from the previous year also is spread on the plots, sometimes several weeks before seeding takes place. There is a wide difference of opinion among farmers as to whether or not seaweed should be put down dry, and, if spread, how long it should be exposed to rain before "rotting" dispels the "juices." The same differences of opinion mark the evaluation of the efficacy of various fertilizers and their use at the several stages of "setting" a garden.

One of the tasks of the agricultural agent is to test soils and advise farmers as to which kinds of seaweed and other fertilizers are best suited for their land. But he seldom is consulted, and if his advice is sought, it is more often than not disregarded. Family and village traditions still guide farming procedures to a great extent, and experimentation is a rarity. Terrace Village farmers employ all four types of seaweed, in part because it is a village custom, but also because they have access to most of the string and black weed in the island. This practice is lauded by the agent as being scientifically the most effective; however, he takes no credit for the Terrace idiosyncracy. Among other important duties performed by

Figure 5. Improving a garden with compost unloaded on seaweed

the agent are providing seed potatoes and overseeing the construction of fences, fields, reservoirs, and outbuildings subsidized by the government.

The average sized farm of a fourth has approximately half of its acreage in quarter- and half-acre gardens; the other half is divided fairly evenly between larger plots containing indigenous soils used for grazing and those enclosing limestone pavement, or "crags." Gardens are smaller in size because subsidies for their manufacture are paid according to the quarter-acre—7 pounds and 10 shillings when a potato crop is grown—and a field this size can be converted into a garden comfortably in the period of a year. Most landholders plant from a half-acre to a full acre of potatoes yearly, and it is estimated that a quarter-acre will produce, under normal weather conditions, nearly four tons of "spuds." According to the agricultural agent, the use of human manure as a fertilizer accounts for such a high yield. The amount of potatoes consumed depends, of course, on the size of the householder's family, but many farmers export surpluses the following summer before new spuds are harvested.

"Improving" refers both to developing a new garden and to enriching an old one with compost (see Fig. 5). New plots usually are manufactured in areas containing indigenous soils, so as to lessen the labor required. If a garden is to be "laid" on pavement, a much fissured area is chosen so that adequate drainage is afforded. The plot is leveled by removing protruding stones with crowbar and sledge hammer (not by throwing a huge boulder from above the head, as shown in the aforementioned film), and fissures are filled with small rocks to the extent that soil components added later will not filter down. Large stones are placed in fences which surround the field, for which the government pays the farmer, or farmers, involved in their construction 2 pounds for each 22 yards raised 4 feet. Writers describing the local milieu seldom fail to mention that fences are numerous and high in Inis Beag so as to prevent the sparse soils from being blown away by Atlantic gales; the truth of the matter is that fences serve as boundaries, are repositories for uprooted rocks that farmers, understandably, do not wish to transport long distances, and by their very construction provide a source of income. Once a field is leveled, it is spread with sand, compost, and sometimes indigenous soils carried from other areas to enrich the new garden. This is a job which is carried on the year around, and children often are pressed into service, loading creels with sand from the strand and common land and driving laden animals to the plots above.

Newly made fields can grow potatoes two years in succession before being fallowed, but old ones must lie fallow four years until the eelworm disappears. The folk, however, plant spuds in their old plots every six to ten years, when moss has accumulated to such a degree that the growth of grass sufficient for grazing and haying is impeded. The potato planting technique is known as the "ridge-and-furrow" or "lazy-bed" method on the mainland, but these terms are not used in Inis Beag. Setting a garden involves first of all constructing parallel "ridges," about 30 inches in width, the length of a field. "Ditches" are dug with a spade, and sods are "turned over" onto strips of seaweed; then more dirt is "trenched" over other seaweed, compost, guano, and chemical fertilizers placed in the center of the ridges (see Fig. 6). The whole procedure is called "manuring," and two months later the garden is again trenched with dirt distributed at the base of the sprouting vines. Between the time of seeding and harvesting, the plot is weeded by hand once or twice and sprayed two or three times with a mixture of copper sulphate and water to combat the potato blight.

Potato seeds are purchased in sacks from the agricultural agent or obtained from the previous year's crop, and it takes almost 100 pounds of seed to plant a

Figure 6. Soil being trenched in setting a garden

quarter-acre garden. The seed potatoes are cut so that each segment has two "eyes," and they are "stabbed" into the ridges in three rows with a digging stick, deep enough to escape the foraging of birds and rats, yet above the decaying seaweed which can "burn" the seed and cause it not to yield. It is not uncommon for women and children to stab seeds while the man of the house is trenching ridges in another part of the field. Many kinds of spuds are grown by the islanders, some of which are "early" and can be harvested before the end of June; the folk argue the relative merits of varieties of potatoes just as they do the use of fertilizers and farming techniques.

Planting must be completed before the cuckoo arrives in late April and sounds its call, and the person who is still seeding when the bird first is heard is the subject of ridicule. The laggard in some parts of Ireland is called a "cuckoo farmer," and it is said in Inis Beag that one who is "lazy about planting is lazy about everything." A tale is told of a Castle villager who saw another man, considered by the islanders to be overly indolent, cutting potato seeds in early April, whereupon he climbed the wall of the castle and imitated the song of the cuckoo. The victim of the practical joke gave up his job in disgust and fed the seed to his poultry. My wife and I witnessed a heated argument in a pub over the date of arrival of the first cuckoo of 1960. Word was passed among the men, some of whom were still planting, that a lighthouse keeper had heard the song five days before. The keeper was denounced as an exaggerator and "troublemaker," and agreement was reached that the bird always is heard first in Low Village and not at the back of the island. The official date of the cuckoo's arrival later was set at April 27th—15 days after its alleged appearance at the lighthouse.

"Late" potatoes are harvested from the ridges by spade as needed from mid-July until the end of October, at which time the gardens are emptied (see Fig. 7). The harvested spuds are separated in the fields into those to be fed to livestock, those to be used for seeding the next year, and those to be eaten; then they are transported by horse or ass to be stored in outbuildings. Just as the person who has failed to complete seeding by the time the cuckoo arrives is censured by his neighbors, so is the one who has not removed all of his potatoes from the ground by mid-November. As a man said to me when evaluating potential sons-in-law, "The father of a girl would think twice about marrying off his daughter to a man who didn't have his spuds in by the middle of the month."

Supplementing the potato dominated diet of the folk are other locally grown vegetables: cabbages, carrots, onions, turnips, parsnips, and lettuce. They are planted between March and May in ridges in much the same manner as spuds—on fallowing land, in small areas within fields containing indigenous soils which have been improved for this purpose, and in gardens in the villages where they are readily accessible. The more prosperous Inis Beag families also avail themselves of canned peas, beans, and carrots sold in the shops. It is usual for men to plant vegetables, but both men and women tend them to maturity and collect the plants after early September as they are needed for the table.

Once the potato fields are emptied, most farmers plant grass in them before the coming of winter. This allows the hay to be cut in June and July of the following year, after which more grass will come in for fall and winter pasturage. Grass

Figure 7. Harvesting spuds near the lake below Terrace Village

seed is thrown out by hand and the top soil turned over by spade to cover it, a task often shared by a man and his offspring. The farmer who wishes to use a plot only for growing hay usually will seed it during the spring after it has yielded spuds and will not permit animals to graze on it until it has been cut and the hay stored. No further seeding is required after the initial one, even though ten years may elapse before potatoes once again are planted.

The tools employed in cutting and stacking hay are the sickle, called a "reaping hook," the scythe, the pitchfork, and the rake. Most are imported, but a few men own handmade rakes whose parts are wooden and fitted together. The farmers substitute wide brimmed felt hats for their usual caps when haying, and do so again a month later when "pulling" rye; the hat is purported to be cooler than the cap and affords protection to the neck of the wearer when he bends over for long spells under a hot sun. Many folk claim that cutting hay is the most strenuous of their jobs on land or sea, but the men work slowly and rest often, just as they do when engaged in other arduous tasks, some of which appear to the outsider to demand a greater output of energy than manipulating a sickle or scythe. Once cut, hay is raked into parallel rows across the field for drying, then formed into cocks, known as "saving the hay," by hand or using a rake, "fork," or scythe. It is possible to stack hay into cocks 24 hours after cutting it, then to transport it to barns and outbuildings after a like period of time (see Fig. 8), but rain and the press of other duties can prolong the operation for as long as two weeks. Seeds for autumn planting are shaken from the hay on the floor of the storage building before the crop is stacked away to furnish winter fodder.

Figure 8. Transporting hay to an outbuilding

Those islanders who dwell in thatched houses or who own other buildings which are thatched grow rye, as do a few farmers who use it as fodder. It is planted in recently dug potato fields at the same time as grass and is ready for harvesting the next August. Rye for thatching is pulled rather than cut, and compressed into small bundles which are propped against fences for drying. Pulling is preferred because grass and weeds can be separated out, and the roots will furnish friction to keep the bundles from slipping when they are placed on the roof later. After drying, the bundles are carried to barns or outbuildings to be flailed, winnowed, and stored until used a month or two afterward. Flailing is done by striking the tops of the bundled plants against a stone placed a foot from an indoor wall, in such a way that the seeds are separated and collected at the base of the wall. Later the grain is spread on a flagging and winnowed by allowing handfuls of seed to fall to the rock surface so that wind blows away the chaff. Rye used as fodder is planted with grass and cut when "green" at the same time that hay is cut, and is handled in almost the same way as the latter.

Care of Livestock

The export of fish, kelp, pigs, cattle, and sheep accounted for 90 percent of the income of Inis Beag folk in 1893, as reported by the Congested Districts Board. The sale of cattle and sheep ranked last, for at that time indigenous soils were not adequate either in extent or grass yield to support many livestock, and fields on the terraces were used mostly for farming. But over the past 70 years kelp-making has disappeared, pig rearing has been abandoned, and fishing has become mainly a subsistence pursuit engaged in by only a small number of islanders. Hand in glove with these developments came the enlargement of arable lands and hence an increase in good pasturage, first necessitated by the intrusion of the eelworm and then stimulated by government agricultural supports. Farming became a more time consuming and lucrative occupation, as did the breeding and fattening of cattle and sheep for export, and the keeping of horses and asses expanded to accommodate the increased emphasis on farming. Thus, while the subsistence economy changed but slightly in two generations, the money economy experienced a radical alteration.

At the present time, 59 householders own one or more cattle; 56, one or more sheep; 22, one or more horses; and 58, one or more asses, among whom 8 have 2 asses and 1 a jennet. The government regulates the breeding of both cattle and horses, with the result that only one man is licensed to own a bull and the horses are mares or geldings. Cows are serviced for a 1 pound stud fee in the most inaccessible of fields, where children and tourists cannot observe the breeding of the "beasts." Most of the asses, just as the bulls and stallions, are castrated, but in this case to prevent them from kicking down fences and braying excessively when sexually aroused. Whereas almost all of the horses and asses and a few cattle have been imported from the mainland, the sheep population is Inis Beag sired. For the most part, cattle are grazed on fallowing plots, the few goats on crags at the back of the island, and other livestock on indigenous pasturage.

Cattle owners usually possess a "milch cow," a yearling, and a calf, and cows and bullocks are sold at two years of age. When a milch cow becomes old and "dried up," it either is fattened and sold or, if the price on the mainland is low, butchered and eaten by the householder and his family, usually between Allhallows and Christmas. "Cattle jobbers" visit the island to purchase cows and bullocks, and in 1960 they were paying between 60 and 80 pounds per beast. Excitement prevails on the strand on days when cattle are shipped off. Each struggling animal is pushed out into the sea by a group of men and then pulled to a canoe by a rope attached around its neck; its head is held over the stern transom of the *curach* for the trip to the steamer, where it is hoisted from the water and swung high over the deck and into a hold. Sometimes an islander is forced by circumstances to import a calf, and in 1960 the purchase price of calves at the fair in a nearby port was approximately 20 pounds; a colt cost about 50 pounds and an ass 5.

Probably the most striking difference between cattle rearing on the mainland and in Inis Beag is that island cows are not stabled, but forage and are milked throughout the year in the fields. Between November and March, they are pastured south of the terrace crest on fallowing and the more luxuriant of the indigenous plots, fed hay and rye carried to them from barns and outbuildings, and watered by bucket from neighboring springs which are swollen from winter rains. Men and boys care for their needs during this period, and often spend as many as three hours walking out and back to the pastures twice each day. With the coming of spring, cows are moved to fields on the terraces where women and children can feed and milk them, or men, who are now entering on the busy agricultural and fishing season, will not use up so much time getting to and from the pastures. Other reasons for shifting cows are that the village wells are more dependable than the springs at the back of the island during occassional summer dry spells, and cows when "tormented" by insects can run about the terrace fields more safely than they can the rockier and more fissured indigenous and improved plots above. Milking is done between eight thirty and ten o'clock in the morning and four thirty and six in the afternoon during the winter, and an hour or two later in the summer. When milking, the farmer crouches at the right side of the beast and holds a pail with his left hand while drawing one teat at a time with his right. He murmurs to the cow in Irish to keep it pacified, and is ready to move swiftly should the animal suddenly shift its position.

To encourage cattle breeding, the government subsidizes the construction of reservoirs at the back of the island for collecting rain water, and of barns and outbuildings for storing hay, rye, potatoes, and farming and fishing equipment. The typical reservoir is placed in an area surrounded by actual or potential grazing land located at a considerable distance from the nearest spring. It is composed of a cemented stone platform with a slanting concave surface which drains into a rectangular shaped tank. Barns and outbuildings are small stone structures, usually thatched, which are single roomed and doored and may have one or two small windows. The barns, like the reservoirs, are placed within easy access of fields used for pasturage.

Sheep are reared in Inis Beag to furnish wool, as well as to be sold and slaughtered for local consumption. They demand little care, as they are allowed to graze in undeveloped pastures and to obtain water from rain filled depressions in the pavement and from plants that they devour. Kept by their owners for five or six years and then disposed of, they are sheared once a year between May and July. There are white, brown, and black haired varieties, and between six and eight pounds of wool can be procured from an animal every shearing. If a householder possesses a large herd, he may choose to sell some of his lambs when they are six months old, and in August many lambs are shipped from Inis Beag on the steamer. Although some folk from time to time slaughter their own sheep to provide meat for the tables, several householders maintain large herds and specialize in selling lamb and mutton to visitors and fellow islanders.

All Inis Beag homes have at least one dog and most of them have a cat. These animals perform certain services and act as pets. At the time walls were low at the back of the island, dogs were employed to round up sheep, and they also aided their owners hunt rabbits along the rock piled shore of the west sound, when the meat of this animal was eaten more commonly than it is today. Now, their duties are restricted to warning of the approach of strangers and chasing chickens out of the kitchen. Cats are kept to catch mice, and their presence on the premises is sufficient to keep rats from approaching the house and outbuildings. They are treated less well than dogs, but both dogs and cats are given little affection and often are not fed enough. It is true that some islanders are strongly attached to their pets and provide them with adequate care, but they are the exceptions. A man devoted to his dog will be followed about the island by the animal, and a desired trait in a dog is that it will not show interest in persons outside of the household. Some cats have reverted to a wild state and roam the back of the island, sheep occasionally are killed by hungry dogs, and young people will entertain themselves by baiting dogs to fight. By and large, animals, especially asses, in Inis Beag are treated roughly or with indifference.

Fishing

It is estimated that between 30 and 50 three-men crews from Inis Beag fished regularly almost the year around at the beginning of the century. At that time there were ten families of fisherfolk—six in Low Village, two in High, and one each in the other two communities—who subsisted mainly on money obtained from the sale of their catches or by bartering fish for needed goods and services. Only farming and kelp-making intermittently interfered with the fishing regime of landholders, and fishing ceased altogether only for parts of December and January, when inclement weather and the Christmas season intruded. Women and children were deeply involved in the fishing endeavor, just as they were in farming and livestock rearing, to free their menfolk for fishing. Crews ranged the coast of Inis Beag and neighboring islands, the two sounds, the mainland coast for 20 miles, and Atlantic shallows 5 to 8 miles offshore. Lines 40 fathoms in length were "shot" for ling and cod, and nets over a mile in length were drifted to ensnare spring mackerel. At times when fish were particularly abundant, fishermen would be out daily for a week or two, arising long before dawn to have their lines down before daybreak, and returning home as late as midnight.

Sixty years later, a sharply contrasting situation prevails, wherein not only has the exporting of fish almost been discontinued, but fish no longer rank as a major staple in the diet of the folk and are not even eaten several months of the year. Nine three-men crews fished fairly regularly with nets and lines between February and October of 1960 and exported or sold locally part of their catches, and two crews fished for lobsters. Fishing now is carried on within a mile of the island, and only one crew ventured as far as the mainland in 1960. It was customary in the past for crews to fish for two consecutive days off a mainland peninsula and sleep overnight in their canoes or lodge in a village there, a venture which required over 30 miles of backbreaking labor at the oars. Line fishing today is done in shallow waters, only short nets are employed, and the men do not care to spend long hours at their task. Elders bemoan the present state of affairs for several reasons, one of them being the loss of fishing lore accumulated over the centuries —knowledge of the ocean floor, of deep currents, of the habitats and movements of fish, not to mention knowledge relating to the manufacture and care of fishing gear and fishing techniques themselves.

Most important of the factors which gradually have restricted fishing are the actions of foreign trawlers—particularly Spanish and French ones, the shift of migratory routes of fish, and long range changes in the weather. During the 1890s, foreign trawlers commenced to fish the waters surrounding Inis Beag, and in the decades since they have increased in number and have fished ever closer to the coast, until now they often penetrate within the legal limit. Not only have

Figure 9. Launching a curach *from the strand in stormy weather*

they taken fish which eventually would have found their way into island nets, but they have destroyed with their trawls spawning beds of certain fish and captured lines and nets set out many miles in the ocean by Inis Beag crews. Another reason why fish have become scarce is that shifting currents or other related factors have caused some fish, especially mackerel, to bypass the region. Other coastal areas of Ireland from which fish seldom were taken in quantity in the past now are thriving, and some islanders look hopefully to the future when once again migratory routes will change and bring the fish back. However, even if fish were more available today, it would be difficult to fish for them from *curach* for part of the year because of worsening weather conditions. Storms have increased in number and severity during the winters, and even the summers which once were relatively "calm" are punctuated with long spells of "rough" weather which makes going out in the canoes risky (see Fig. 9). Finally, a seldom admitted factor also must be considered—the indolence of the men. Aged fishermen assert that sufficient fish are still available to make serious fishing a highly profitable occupation, but that young men have been "spoiled" by government benevolence and are unwilling to undergo the hardships entailed—"Why rise before dawn and row all day when you can draw the dole?" During 1959, those crews which fished the most averaged between 50 and 60 pounds per man for the season.

Whereas the efforts of the Irish Free State and the Republic to improve Inis Beag living standards have been directed mostly toward stimulating agriculture and animal husbandry, those of the government before 1922 were focused on making fishing a more productive enterprise. The Congested Districts Board introduced trawlers and other types of fishing vessels and financed their purchase by islanders of the region, sent instructors to teach fishermen how to use the new boats and gear, set up curing and storage facilities in the islands, facilitated the shipping of fish to mainland markets, and attempted to regulate these markets so as to ensure maximum profits for the folk. These efforts failed for the most part in Inis Beag, and today the men fish from *curach*, much as did their grandfathers. The continuing effort of the government to improve fishing in the area is reflected in instruction in modern fishing techniques at a school in a nearby island, and the successful operation of a number of government financed trawlers and other fishing boats from there.

The islanders consider fish from the sea, which are netted, more palatable and healthier to eat than those caught with lines and trawls, fresh water fish, and fish which have been cured or frozen. Fish taken on lines, because they bleed, and those enmeshed in trawls, because they suffocate, are thought to suffer in taste and nourishment, as do those which are treated artificially for sale; and fresh water fish are believed to be unhealthy to eat because they feed on refuse thrown into lakes and rivers rather than on natural foods. Some folk exclude even mackerel from their diet, since these fish "swim on the surface and eat everything dirty afloat." We already have noted that Inis Beag elders prefer seaweed to chemical fertilizers; the preference for netted fish which feed on natural foods to fresh water fish and mackerel which are contaminated is another example of a recurrent cultural theme—the positive valuation of natural objects and the negative valuation of artificial ones which come in contact with the human body. Other manifestations of this theme are the emphasis placed on folk medicines and the distrust of medicines prescribed by nurse and doctor, the belief that certain foods will assure health and combat specific illnesses, and the fear of piped water and canned foods. I often was told that I could improve my eyesight by giving up my glasses and rubbing dew on my eyelids, or by walking along the seashore to allow the wind and spray to penetrate my eyeballs.

Over 30 varieties of fish are caught off Inis Beag, some with lines of varying length and number of hooks, others in the four types of nets, and a few with both lines and nets. Most important of the fish are: ling, cod, bream, gurnet, haddock, and autumn mackerel caught with lines; plaice, turbot, rock fish, and pollack both netted and taken on lines; and herring and spring mackerel captured in special nets. Trammel and drag nets are used in addition to herring and mackerel nets, and the most commonly used baits are gurnet, haddock, conger eel, bream, herring, and limpets. Fishing techniques vary considerably, as do the times of the year when particular kinds of fish are available, the localities that they frequent, and the baits which are most effective for each variety. Fishing crews form at different times of the year, often to fish in certain areas for specific fish. They are composed of both kin and close friends, and they tend to alter in membership from year to year as other activities intrude.

Before I leave the subject of fishing, I wish to correct three commonly held misconceptions concerning Inis Beag men: they are all skilled seamen; because they spend much of their time at sea they are of necessity able swimmers; and many of them have lost their lives to the ocean. Islanders are well aware of the wide differences in rowing and fishing abilities among themselves, and the evaluation of the skills of various men, past and present, is a much heard subject of conversation. Also, many men choose not to fish because they are unable to develop the requisite talents, are prone to severe seasickness, or are overly wary of the dangers associated with fishing. It seems reasonable to assume that people who spend so much time on the water as a matter of safety will have learned to swim, but I was unable to discover a single islander who possesses this skill. The reasons put forward to account for the fact are several, but the most significant one never is broached—the puritanical reluctance to bare the body either publicly or privately at any age. Folk rationalizations are best summed up in the following quotations: "Nothing will happen to the man who knows the sea.", "Better for a man to drown at once and save himself the suffering.", "The man who can't swim will take more care.", and "When death is on a man, he can't be saved."

A recurring motif in writings about Inis Beag is the threatening sea and heavy loss of life among fishermen, with its attendant psychological depression. In the past century, only four sea accidents have occurred in the island with the loss of but 12 lives. The folk are extremely cautious out of respect for the elements, handle their canoes with remarkable dexterity, and are excellent weather forecasters. The claim of one famous writer that each family has lost male members to the ocean reflects not only his psychological outlook, but the breadth and depth of kinship reckoning and the high degree of inbreeding—as an islander told me, "Every Inis Beag family is related, and the drowned man might have been eight-of-kin (third cousin) who died 60 years ago." The motif can be attributed to the projection of a tragic world view into the interpretation of the local culture by some authors, to the nativistic and primitivistic biases of other writers, and to a common sense conclusion reached by observers who have spent little time in the island and have failed to "count noses."

Diet

The diet of the islanders is simple, and only one large meal is eaten during the day. After the turf fire is rekindled from coals and water is boiled for tea, the family assembles for a breakfast which includes bread spread with butter and jam and tea mixed with ample amounts of milk and sugar. Dinner at noon and lunches in the late afternoon and before retiring at night feature the same ingredients, although a boiled or fried egg usually is added to the dinner menu. The supper, eaten between seven and eight o'clock in the summer and an hour or two earlier during the winter, is the main meal when the family once again is united, and at this time boiled potatoes and vegetables, and meat if available, dominate the menu. Again bread and tea are served, and a dessert, or "sweet"—such as custard, rhubarb, blancmange, or biscuits—may be added. Children of school age in a family eat together at noon and after school and may be joined by their father, but his duties often absent him from one or both of these meals, and he may carry bread and tea with him while fishing or be brought his dinner and afternoon lunch in the field. Infants and young children are fed milk at various times, and the youth often eat biscuits, candy, or bread spread with sugar between the five regular meals.

Most women bake their own bread in "pot ovens" suspended over the open fire, with ingredients purchased in the shops, but some buy bakery bread which is delivered from the mainland once a week. Women with many offspring must bake bread daily, since as many as five loaves will be eaten in a day by a family of eight. Cream is saved from the milk and turned into butter in locally made churns every few days, to provide the pound or more of butter consumed in a week by each member of the family. A few women purchase shop butter and also margarine for cooking, but the latter is not used on the table (despite the fact that it is one-third the price of imported butter), because it is an artificial product and thus thought to lack food value. Both chicken and duck eggs are eaten, and some persons prefer hard to soft boiled eggs. Men insist on drinking their tea from large mugs and prefer their bread sliced thick and spread generously with butter. Telling of a tea that he attended in Dublin, a man complained of teacups the size of egg cups and bread cut so thin that "you could see houses on the mainland through it." Children are more prone than adults to use jam on their bread, and a large jar of imported jam will last but a day in a household containing six children.

Few families can afford to serve meat daily, and sometimes several days will pass before meat appears on the table. Among the meats eaten are lamb, mutton, chicken, and fish procured locally, and rasher and sausage bought in the shops; however, some families have beef and lamb shipped directly to them from mainland shops weekly. Meats usually are boiled, even fish, and soup and gravy are made from the liquids formed. Although lobsters, crabs, snails, and other shelled sea creatures are obtained by the folk, they are exported, used for bait, or cast aside rather than eaten. Two kinds of seaweed are included in the diet and are considered delicacies: creannach, which can be consumed raw as it is pulled but more commonly is boiled and dried before being eaten, and carraigín, which when cooked with milk makes a tasty blancmange. These seaweeds are believed to promote health and are used as folk medicines by some islanders, who regard them as having a magical potency.

The potatoes grown in Inis Beag are considered outstanding in taste, even when compared with those grown on the mainland. They are boiled in a "cooking pot" over the open hearth; this container is deeper and has a rounder bottom than its pot oven counterpart. At one time, it was customary to drain potatoes and eat them from a round, flat, short-sided basket woven from sally rods, called a ciseog. They still are drained with the basket in many households, but I have observed only three families eating communally from a ciseog atop the table. This is thought to be a "backward" custom, and a film producer earned the wrath of the folk by portraying this trait in his work; actually, it did not appear in the film, nor did other sequences, such as a women suckling a pig in time of drought, which the islanders claim that the producer included to brand them "savages." Potatoes when eaten are "stabbed" with a fork, peeled with a knife, and eaten with the fork. It is not unusual for a man to eat six or eight large spuds at a sitting, and the pot used to boil potatoes for a large family is piled high indeed. Spuds also are fed to cattle, poultry, and pets. The diet of families which are most prosperous, keep tourists, or whose members are acculturated is more varied than the diet that I have just described, and these families utilize the shops more than is usual.

The excessive intake of carbohydrates, particularly by children, coupled with the almost complete absence of dental hygiene, has resulted in universal tooth decay among the folk. Many people in their twenties and thirties already wear false teeth, and toothache is the most common physical ailment. My wife and I discovered but one adult who cleans her teeth, and she only once a week with a cloth and toothpaste. The islanders eschew use of the toothbrush for several reasons: some believe that bad teeth are inherited or decay is a contagious disease, and nothing can be done to prevent deterioration once it has set in; others equate decay with the common cold, a natural affliction suffered by everyone which must be accepted fatalistically (and masochistically); while still others regard the tooth-brush as an English innovation or its use as an upper class affectation—"If I used one they would say I had fancy ideas."—to be shunned on these grounds. A story whose plot was laid in an island in the region of Inis Beag appeared in the *Saturday Evening Post*, and was illustrated with photographs taken in Inis Thiar. The Dublin model who portrayed the heroine in local attire was recognized as an outsider by the folk who viewed the pictures because her teeth were white and even.

Clothing

The term traditional applied to the much publicized Inis Beag garb refers to the homespun vests and trousers and blue woolen shirts of the men, the ankle-length red and blue woolen skirts and a type of shawl of the women, and the cowskin shoes and woven belts worn by many men but only a few women. Some of these articles of wear are shared with peasants of the region, or were in the past and thus are vestigial; others are unique to Inis Beag; and all are in the process of being replaced by mass produced mainland attire. Of 111 adult males in Inis Beag, 11 have given up the local dress, as have 9 of the 85 adult females. Most of these 20 have returned to the island from having spent time on the mainland or abroad, and as a matter of prestige have chosen to retain the foreign costume. Practically all of the young men past school age who have not been away dress traditionally, but none of the women between ages 18 and 29 do; the youngest women who wear the red or blue skirt are of the latter age.

Although most clothing worn by the islanders is tailored locally, everything but the trousers and vests of the men are made from imported materials. Clothing is tailored from cloth woven by the island weaver from Inis Beag wool which is washed, dyed, and spun in the homes but carded on the mainland. The trousers are brown or grey depending on whether a brown or black weft is combined with the white warp on the loom; they are called "britches" when styled differently as to seam and hem. Vests also are brown or grey in front with backs dyed blue, and are worn over dark colored sweaters or blue woolen pullover shirts. Most sweaters are imported, although some of simple design are knitted by women, and shirts are sewn from wool sold in the shops. Under the outer layer of clothing are worn lightweight grey woolen undershirts, known as "grey shirts," and heavier white woolen—"bawneen"—underpants, called "white drawers." The grey shirt is flannel, but the folk use that term to designate homespun wool. Sometimes a bawneen waistcoat is substituted for the vest, and in the heat of the summer may be worn directly over the undershirt. Making up the remainder of the male costume are the ubiquitous Irish visored cap, imported leather or locally manufactured belts and shoes, and stockings. One of the most time consuming chores of women is knitting and darning stockings for their husbands and children.

Just as the vest is the most striking item of male apparel, the red or blue skirt, or "petticoat," is the most striking female one, in particular the red petticoat when viewed from afar against the dull colors of sand and limestone. The skirt, made from imported wool but dyed locally, is gathered and styled with a deep tuck about nine inches from the bottom, and under this in winter is worn an additional bawneen or red skirt. Sometimes a cotton petticoat and knee length "knickers" also are worn, and several layers of cotton "vests" and shirts provide needed warmth beneath the cotton or lightweight woolen handmade blouse during winter. Blouses are styled alike with collars, long sleeves, and buttons down the front, and usually are of subdued plaid material purchased in the shops. However, somewhat unusual designs and colors are admired, as are brooches worn at the neck of the garment. Black knee length woolen stockings and black leather shoes, both procured in the shops, encase the feet. Over the shoulders may be worn a multi-colored or red island crocheted shawl of small size, called a "shawleen." In winter and when attending church, women wear heavy brown woolen paisley or black shawls outdoors which cover the head. The black shawl can be bought on the mainland, but the paisley shawl is no longer available.

Infants of both sexes until toilet trained are clothed in plain bawneen dresses. Then boys don short pants of varying length made from homespun wool, which are worn with white sweaters or blue shirts. Corduroy trousers and jackets are coming into vogue for everyday wear, but on Sunday the white sweater always is worn. Older boys wear long woolen trousers or britches and blue shirts, and children of all ages go barefooted or put on sandals during the summer and add hand knit stockings in winter. Girls past infancy wear frocks sewn by their mothers, bought in the shops, or sent by relatives from abroad. Whether shoes and stockings are worn depends on the weather, and girls don sweaters and coats over their dresses to afford them protection against the cold. Hairbows provide the only decoration.

Underclothing is changed once a week, and women try to wash clothes that often as well. A man has at least one old and one new vest, trousers, and shirt, and on Sunday and for special events he will wear his newest articles of clothing; the same can be said of women's petticoats and accouterments. Winter and summer attire remains the same for both sexes except that some underclothing is shed during the summer, and at night on retiring outer clothing is removed and some underclothing retained. The latter practice reflects extreme modesty as well as the need for warmth. Islanders have an obsessive fear of nakedness which permits them, after infancy, to bathe only their feet, hands, and face and precludes bathing in the sea and the use of bathtubs.

Crafts

Of the several crafts practiced in Inis Beag, only three are strictly income instead of combined subsistence-income activities: the manufacture of *curach* by four men, the mass production of stockings by four girls in the factory at the coast guard station, and the fashioning of miniature canoes by a single man. Sweaters, woven belts, cowhide shoes, and the small multi-colored shawls are made both for local wear and for export. Most of the exported sweaters are sold to a particular mainland firm for resale, as are all of the model canoes, and the factory is sponsored by Gaeltacht Eireann which markets the stockings produced. Other craft commodities are sold by the folk directly to consumers, most of whom are tourists.

The long rowing canoe of Inis Beag is distributed widely along the west coast of Ireland, from Cos. Donegal to Kerry, and its seaworthy qualities as well as the rowing skill of the crews which sail it are renowned. One of a number of varieties of the coracle, which has a heritage extending back to the Mesolithic, it is built of deal and oak lathes and covered with tarred canvas (see Fig 10). Before canvas was introduced, untanned seal, cow, and horse hides were used for covering, and these were reported from a nearby island less than 100 years ago. The *curach* is approximately 20 feet in length, has a high pointed nose, is round bellied and lacks a keel, draws less than 6 inches of water, and is rowed with narrow 10-feet-long oars. These oars are bladeless for use in rough seas and are pivoted on single tholepins rather than in oarlocks. The looms of the oars overlap, so that oarsmen must pull cross-handed, and on long journeys a lug sail is hoisted to relieve the crew. For the neophyte, rowing a *curach* cross-handed in a heavy sea can be even more abusive of the hands than rebuilding a gateway in a stone fence. Most canoes hold three men—are "three-oared"—but two-, four-, and even five-men *curach* were or are used. Loads up to a ton and a half can be accommodated, and trussed asses, sheep, and horses sometimes are transported in them.

Forty-two householders in Inis Beag own three-men canoes, among whom three have additional two-oared *curach*. The craft are stored upside down in "cots" on either side of the strand along the margins of the common land, although Terrace villagers use a small beach along the northeast coast of the island; they are carried between the cots and the water upside down on the shoulders of the crew, and in that position resemble gigantic beetles. Two Inis Beag men are at work building canoes most of the time, and when they are not busy at this task they construct furniture for local sale. Two other men manufacture *curach* occasionally, and another two who once built them have discontinued the practice. No canoe makers are found elsewhere in the region; therefore, Inis Beag artisans serve the

Figure 10. Assembling lathes in the construction of a canoe

folk of neighboring islands as well as mainland seamen for many miles around. A *curach* takes a week of steady work to construct, and the builder is paid 6 pounds for his labor and a shopkeeper 12 pounds for the materials.

The curate blesses a newly manufactured canoe, and a small bottle of holy water is kept in its bow to afford the crew magical protection. Some fishermen seek further spiritual assistance by tipping their caps and making the sign of the cross with salt water before shoving off, especially if they are about to encounter hazardous weather conditions or are to make a long voyage. One of the many omens known to the folk is a "prayer to guide you safely," passed down from the time of St. Patrick, it is claimed, which is uttered by fishermen ready to put out to sea; if two mistakes are made in its recitation, danger is in the offing and the trip is postponed or cancelled. Another sign of impending peril which will cause postponement of a fishing trip is for one of the crew to meet a red-haired woman on the trail as he walks to the strand to embark.

The knit sweater, called a "ganzie," is not a traditional item of wear, as is commonly asserted by writers, but was introduced in the 1890s as a cottage industry by the Congested Districts Board, which sent instructors to Inis Beag to teach the women there the manner of knitting the intricate patterns. Only children wear the ganzie, for men always have preferred a dark sweater of simple design which is indigenous to the island. The patterns bear such euphonious names as "crooked road," "figure eight," "double diamond," "rosebud," "honeycomb," and "blackberry," and most of them are common to the rest of Ireland, the British Isles, and other parts of Europe. The term ganzie, in fact, undoubtedly derives from the Channel island, Guernsey. A widely held belief that each Inis Beag family has its own distinctive sweater pattern, comparable to the Scottish tartan, by which its drowned members are identified is unfounded. Seventeen women knit for the mainland company, which supplies them with yarn, and are paid between 2 pounds and 2 pounds and 10 shillings by weight for each sweater. Some are able to knit a ganzie in a week, but others take two or three weeks; one woman made 41 sweaters during 1959. A girl working steadily at the knitting factory can earn slightly more in a week than one knitting a ganzie in that time, but most girls choose to knit sweaters because they can be at home where their task seems less tedious. Some women prefer to sell their sweaters to tourists and can on occasion dispose of a ganzie for as much as 6 pounds, but these women must purchase their own yarn, and marketing is much less secure as tourists seldom come into island homes. At present, the finest ganzies are knitted by women in Co. Donegal, a fact which Inis Beag women admit privately.

The woven belt and cowhide shoes of Inis Beag folk have an ancient heritage, just as has the *curach*. It is not known when the belt, or *crios*, was introduced into Ireland, but it has been worn for centuries by Portuguese seamen. Known as "pampooties," the island style footwear once was worn widely in Ireland, although made from various hides and skins, and a century ago was cut from sealskin in Inis Beag. The term pampootie is of Scandinavian origin, and my wife and I have heard it used among Danish peasants to describe their shoes. Today, a Danish expatriate who has lived in the island for almost a decade supports himself by weaving *crios* on a loom for the folk; he also sells them to visitors and to mainland shops along with woven ties and bookmarks. Although "the Dane" has come to monopolize the production of belts, several women occasionally make them by hand for their menfolk and to sell. The manufacture of *crios* once was largely in the hands of women, and they wore them sewn to their petticoats and tied at the side, but now it is mostly men who wear them. Three yards long and two inches wide, the belt is woven with a multitude of colors and designs and is worn wrapped twice around the body and tucked in at either side of the waist. Elders prefer traditional designs and shun the color green because it is unlucky, but young men are coming to like experimental patterns and all of the basic colors and their many shades. Contrary to popular opinion, there are no family designs. Some persons, however, ask for the same pattern every two or three years when they buy a new *crios* if they believe that it has brought them luck.

Pampooties are favored in Inis Beag because they are ideally suited for wet rocks and frail canoes. The spiked heels of female tourists and visiting emigrants who come ashore in *curach* are viewed with trepidation by crewmen, who are supported on the sea only by thin canvas. Most men are able to make pampooties for themselves, but several islanders specialize in the craft and sell their wares to their fellows and to visitors. Usually cured hides are imported from the mainland, and 40 pairs of pampooties can be fashioned from a whole cowhide. They are cut to shape the foot, have the hair outside, are secured front and back by lacing, and when used daily will last about two months. To be pliable, they must be kept moist, so they are dipped in water when they become dry and hardened; however, because they are worn constantly in wet grass and sand, they seldom lose their softness.

In this chapter, I have considered all of the important means of gaining a livelihood in Inis Beag. Some I have discussed at length, while others I have touched on briefly and will reconsider later; but two thus far not referred to—piloting and recovering objects washed ashore—I would like to take up before ending the chapter. Only one pilot remains in the island, but early in the century men of several families guided vessels through the east sound to ports on the mainland. Then it was customary to place lookouts at the high points of Inis Beag to scan the horizon for masts of approaching ships, and often several canoes would race miles out to sea in order to be first to contact a potential customer. The Terrace villager who still plies the trade seldom contacts likely vessels now, and more often than not his services are refused once he rows to a ship, what with modern charts and navigating instruments. Piloting is still very much alive in the memories of the folk, and one of the popular genres of folklore is the humorous anecdote dealing with real and imagined experiences of pilots. One of these concerns a crew fishing in the east sound which was hailed by the captain of a passing schooner. Although not a pilot, an old member of the crew claimed that he was and climbed aboard, and the captain agreed to hire him after he said that he knew the sound and coastline well. Soon after, the ship struck bottom "with a great bump," and the enraged captain shouted, "I thought you said you knew all the rocks in the sound.", to which the islandman replied in a quiet voice, "I did, and that's one of them." The same old man in another tale earns the job by boxing the compass in Gaelic for the captain; the humor of this story lies in the fact that the captain does not know Irish, and the islandman, who in turn does not know the points of the compass, simply recites terms of reference[2] for kin in a rhythmic manner.

One of the oldest of Inis Beag traditions is the "law of wrack"—the right of islanders to confiscate objects of value which have washed ashore. If a person discovers wrack, he establishes ownership by placing a stone atop it or by carrying it above high water mark, and no one else will claim it. Some islanders wander along the shores at dawn seeking what objects may have washed in during the night, especially timber, and those who habitually engage in this pursuit are known disparagingly as "wrack-boomers"—so poor that they must depend on salvage. During the two world wars, the economy of Inis Beag was bolstered by the immense amount of wreckage which drifted in from torpedoed ships, and the islanders still reminisce about particular visitations of flour, planks, and other

---

[2] See p. 75 for a definition of terms of reference.

valuable commodities. Vessels which have run aground in the past have been stripped, and in 1960 a portion of the stricken freighter's cargo—namely Scotch whiskey, yarn, boiler pipes, toilet fixtures, sacks, shoes, and other goods—was obtained by the folk under the law of wrack. The importance and tenacity of the law were attested by the fact that "salvaging" was continued in the face of opposition from ship owners, insurance representatives, customs officials, visiting police, and even the imprecations of curate and parish priest.

3

The Village and the Family

Village Differences

LOW VILLAGE RECEIVES ITS NAME from its position on the lowest terrace of Inis Beag (see Fig. 4). It borders the ocean and strand, while High Village to the east is located in a wide expanse south of the common land formed by a concavity in the upper terraces. On the western of the two promontories high above the beach, separated from Low and Terrace by rift valleys, is Castle Village. Below it are the cemetery enclosing the church of the patron saint and the new school, and above it are the castle, the ruined monastery, the Napoleonic watch tower, and what remains of the old school next to the tower. The Ordnance Survey Maps place the highest elevation of Inis Beag in the vicinity of the tower, but the folk claim that the most elevated portion of the crest is above High. Terrace Village, on the promontory to the east, presents a breath-taking view of the lake (see Fig. 7), the sound, and towering mountains and cliffs along the mainland coast. Low merges with High, but Castle and Terrace, because they are located on high terraces and bounded by rift valleys, are isolated units. Terrace is aligned north and south, but the other three settlements are aligned roughly east and west. The southernmost house of Terrace and the westernmost one of Low are approximately 1500 yards apart, and the intervening distance can be walked comfortably in less than 12 minutes.

Below are the number of inhabited houses and the population of each village:

	Houses	*Population*
Low Village	24	119
High Village	16	59
Castle Village	17	99
Terrace Village	14	73

It is apparent from the size of these settlements that some such term as hamlet might be more appropriate than village, but I have chosen to follow island usage. Within each village, no house is further than 50 yards from its nearest neighbor, some even sharing the same gable, and a myriad of paths serve to link single and grouped dwellings with a main road.

Although the traditions of Inis Beag and islands in its vicinity can be designated as a subculture of the Irish system taken as a whole, nevertheless there are marked differences in custom between them. One might suppose that cultural variation would be slight in an island as small and stable as Inis Beag, but the remarkable fact is that there are differences among the four villages. The folk are well aware of inter-village, inter-island, and island-mainland cultural variability, and they also possess a well defined image of their own way of life. At this point, I would like to examine the attitudes of the people toward their own communities, Inis Thiar, the mainland, themselves, and outsiders who visit or live among them.

High and Castle Villages attract the fewest opinions. The inhabitants of the former are accused of arriving late at island affairs, especially to mass in the chapel so close at hand, and dwellers in the latter of keeping ferocious dogs which bark at night and molest visitors. Until recently, each Castle household had from two to four dogs, and it was possible for those living in Low to know when a visitor making a night visit had arrived in Castle by the outcry of the animals. Castle people, like those in Terrace, milk their cows earlier in the day than do other islanders, and since both settlements are located on the upper terraces and command exceptional views of the mainland coast and sea around, the dwellers in each claim that their panorama is the most inspiring.

The numerous attitudes toward Low and Terrace Villages mostly reflect their positions in the island and resultant differential acculturation; generally speaking, the local culture becomes more traditional as one moves eastward from Low, the jetty, and the strand. It is often said that Terrace folk "are strangers to the rest of us" and resemble the inhabitants of Inis Thiar, whom many writers and scientists claim are the most traditional of Irish peasants. More cottages are thatched and the indigenous costume is more in evidence in Terrace than elsewhere, and the villagers there are the earliest risers and hardest workers and tend to arrive early for events, in contradistinction to their High neighbors. Families in Terrace are considered more closely knit and cooperative and the people more self-reliant than those in the other communities. The men spend less time in the pubs, do not need drink to "give them courage" to sing and dance, and are livelier and more extroverted at parties. Not only do Terrace folk believe that their village is best located as to beauty of land and seascape, but they claim that it is quieter and the air is healthier there than elsewhere in Inis Beag. Another Terrace custom often cited is that of farmers using all four types of seaweed as fertilizers and setting their gardens in the same manner; farmers in the other settlements use only two or three kinds of seaweed and set their gardens in a variety of ways. Lastly, the practice of seeking wrack is most prevalent among Terrace men. The freighter ran aground near Terrace, and the men there were said to have acquired more salvage than other islanders as a result of their being close to the ship and inveterate wrack-boomers. The separateness of Terrace villagers was made most apparent at the time of the shipwreck through the aggression, both overt and covert, directed against them by their fellows.

The behavior of Low villagers, on the other hand, is often the opposite of that of Terrace people less than a mile away; for instance, the folk of Low are the latest risers and milkers, the least industrious, and the most prone to spend time in the pubs. They claim to be descendants of the earliest immigrants in the seventeenth century and are the most boastful of family genealogies. However, most of the landless householders live in Low and as such are held in low repute by landed villagers. People here are the most receptive to tourists, and the two pubs which attract outsiders and the several private homes in which tourists may lodge all are located in Low. It is said that Terrace folk do not need and are indifferent to tourists, whereas Low villagers could not survive without them, either economically or psychologically. Although islanders today visit nearby islands and the mainland less than did their forebears at the turn of the century, the people of Low are considered the most traveled, past and present, of the local population.

As for attitudes directed outward, most islanders regard the culture of Inis Thiar as more traditional than their own. Often heard is the assertion that 70 years ago the inhabitants of the two islands were almost alike as to behavior and beliefs, but the coming of lighthouse and coast guard families, and a permanent curate after 1919, to Inis Beag introduced successive changes which gradually widened the cultural gap between the two. Another factor of importance hindering acculturation in Inis Thiar has been its lack of good landing facilities for visitors to come ashore; the steamer must stand off the jetty of Inis Thiar in the unprotected and often turbulent sound and be met by canoes, whereas it can approach closely the strand of Inis Beag, between the jetty and a point of land, where under most weather conditions it is relatively calm.

Visitors to Inis Beag also hold the same opinion of the two cultures, and the most often made comparison between the islands is the Irish spoken in them. The people of Inis Beag and Inis Thiar recognize slight differences in vocabulary, grammar, and pronunciation between the two speech communities, but they seldom rank their respective proficiencies, unless outsiders in one island assert that the Gaelic spoken in the other is "purer." Once a tourist angered visiting Inis Thiar fishermen in my presence by publicly pronouncing that the Irish in Inis Beag is superior, and that he would send his children here to learn Gaelic and then to Inis Thiar to learn English; the tongue-in-check statement was prompted by a discussion of the linguistic skills of the publican in the neighboring island, who is called "the English speaker" because of the rapidity of his speech and chronic misuse of esoteric English words. Indigenous nativists are far more numerous and militant in Inis Thiar than in Inis Beag, and the anger of the fishermen reflected pride in their own culture and their belief that it is more traditional than that of Inis Beag.

Inis Thiar folk are thought by their neighbors to the east to be more industrious and extroverted than themselves. They are believed to rise earlier, work longer and more energetically with fewer breaks for contemplation or gossip with passersby, and live more frugally and save more as a result. Gruff, impatient, and often impolite, they talk rapidly in high pitched voices and shout at their beasts and at one another from a distance, and on occasion they will use profanity. Inis Thiar men drink more than Inis Beag men, it is claimed; rather than sipping slowly and savoring their stout and whiskey, they consume it quickly and are more concerned with the effects that it produces. It is admitted in Inis Beag that all Irish are inquisitive and disposed to gossip about their fellows, but islanders to the west are openly so and will "demand" information from tourists and will discuss one another quite freely. Braver, "bolder," and less concerned with morality, men from Inis Thiar rowed to the freighter on several occasions and contested successfully with local folk for salvage, which caused some Inis Beag wives to deride their husbands for not possessing these qualities. Women of Inis Thiar also are thought to be braver and bolder, and remain less in their homes, visit relatives and acquaintances and the shops more often, and in general participate more in social events than do their sisters to the east. Despite being extremely critical of Inis Thiar folk for possessing the above and many other less prominent traits, the people of Inis Beag grudgingly admit that their neighbors possess greater *esprit de corps* and enjoy life more than themselves. Once a person emigrates from Inis Beag, he or she seldom returns; but Inis Thiar emigrants are "clever" and do well abroad, and often return with earnings to remain at home, especially women who come back with "fortunes" to seek husbands.

The attitudes of islanders toward those living on the mainland—"townspeople" or "city folk"—reveal a primitivistic bias which probably can be traced back to the Viking occupation, when towns first were established in Ireland and primitive Celts became transformed into peasants: "that primitive people retain a morality which civilized people tend to lose; that a man's moral worth declines in rough proportion to his distance from the soil; that civilization must be held accountable for man's noteworthy catalogue of vices;" (Ardrey 1961:147–148). Inis Beag folk regard themselves as impeccably moral and mainlanders, although fellow Catholics, as immoral; yet the "progressiveness" of the latter is envied secretly and gives rise to the sensitivity of islanders to the real and imagined denigration of them by mainlanders for their backwardness. Mainland Irish are thought to be overly pecuniary, dishonest, rude, and promiscuous. When visiting towns and cities on the mainland, Inis Beag people for many years have worn mainland attire so as not to be singled out and ridiculed. They are ashamed of their English speech—even though adults speak the tongue with greater proficiency than many urban dwellers—and believe that they are prey to dishonest shopkeepers, who are ever ready to take advantage of their ignorance and naiveté. Whenever my wife and I paid short visits to a nearby port or to Dublin, we were requested by islanders to make purchases, have repairs made under our name, and transact other business for them because we were "too clever to be cheated." Once in the city, the folk miss Inis Beag with its clear air and broad expanses, and they complain of the tall buildings (seldom more than four stories high) which "press in" on them, the bustle of the main street, the curious stares of townspeople, and the dirtiness of buildings and roads. In claiming that few islanders would prefer to live there by choice, an old woman said, "City folk are always troubled. They aren't their own bosses, and they get up too early and work too hard. They face the dangers of traffic, and, worst of all, they meet with temptations of the flesh."

In the last chapter, I discussed two facets of the Inis Beag self-image: their seldom admitted poverty and indolence. Other facets have just been revealed in their appraisals of various groups, and still more are apparent when one examines their attitudes toward visitors to the island. During the summer, they enjoy the presence of strangers on the strand at steamer time, in the pubs, and at parties, and when winter comes many conversations dwell on those who were "great gas" —entertaining in song, dance, or repartee. But outsiders fulfill a far deeper need, in that most of them express admiration for the island and its inhabitants. They praise the beauty, antiquities, and history of Inis Beag, but more importantly the friendliness of the people and those customs and personality traits publicized by writers and film producers, which are "discovered" even when nonexistent or considerably "diluted." Departing tourists usually vow that they will return, and they are asked repetitiously what it was that so pleased them and if they will be "lonesome after they leave." Reflected here are the profound feelings of inferiority of the folk and their need for constant reassurance of their worth. Much of the depression among islanders during winter months is related to the absence of outsiders who stimulate them and are subjects of gossip.

The people of Inis Beag regard themselves as friendly, polite, and hospitable to outsiders—not at all like their Inis Thiar neighbors, who are said not to like tourists and to extort money from them for giving information and allowing themselves to be photographed. Strangers never are derided for behaving in a disapproved fashion but are "treated with dignity," although some men will try to gain free drinks and other favors from outsiders in a calculating and beguiling manner (called "being cute" in Ireland), which is frowned on by the majority of folk. During the summer when tourists are plentiful, many islanders behave according to the nativistic and primitivistic expectations of the strangers: attire becomes more traditional and newer costumes are worn, canoes are rowed with greater vigor, conversations become more boastful, and the like. The sensitivity of the islanders to nativism and primitivism is quite selective, however, in that they extol certain of their indigenous customs and are ashamed of others. Actions which give credence to such character traits as spirituality, strength, and courage are exaggerated, while those which belie such traits as independence, self-reliance, and industriousness are carefully hidden. My wife and I kept a careful record of the responses of Inis Beag folk to questions that we posed concerning their history and culture when we first visited the island in 1958. More than 40 replies turned out to be erroneous, and some of them would have done credit to the most ardent nativist or primitivist.

Most tourists who visit Inis Beag share a mystique fostered by interpretations of island life in the works of writers and film producers. A similar mystique is found elsewhere in the world among idealized primitive and peasant peoples. In Inis Beag, it often causes visitors to seek acceptance from the folk, to resent the presence of other outsiders, to boast of their intimate knowledge of Inis Beag customs and, in some cases, to "go native" in so far as circumstances permit.

Strangers who spend weeks or months in Inis Beag and are able to grasp some of the realities of life there often leave emotionally distraught, knowing that they never will be accepted by the people. Acceptance by the islanders is a problem faced by not only outsiders, but by immigrants. The latter remain strangers for two or three generations, and some people, particularly descendants of fisherfolk, are regarded as outsiders despite the fact that the families of some have resided in Inis Beag for almost a century. Later we will learn that the islanders have difficulty forming affectional bonds among themselves, even among kin; thus, they are able to give even less of themselves to those "who do not belong." Strangers who know Inis Beag well often complain that they must do all of the "giving," as the folk can only "take."

The islanders also share attitudes toward other individuals and groups, which I can mention only in passing. Among the most important are those concerning outsiders who have lived in Inis Beag for long periods of time (the expatriate Dane, lighthouse keepers, Brendan Behan the writer, and Siobhain McKenna the actress); writers who have composed works about the island and have dwelled there or are folk themselves; particular persons from Inis Thiar and other nearby islands (a policeman, a teacher, a man of great strength, a keeper of a guest house, and a man who provides taxi service between the islands and the mainland in a small boat); peasants from bordering counties; religious groups (Protestants generally, members of the Church of Ireland, Jews, and even Italian Catholics); ethnic and racial groups (Americans, English, Germans, Negroes, tinkers, and foreigners as a class); and, finally, politicians and government bureaucrats and the Irish press.

I know of but few cases of discrimination practiced against any of these, but prejudices held against some of them abound, based either on historical experiences (with the English and the Church of Ireland) or on views inculcated by returned emigrants (concerning Jews and Negroes, who seldom visit Inis Beag). Islanders, as well as most Irish, are ambivalent about "Yanks," as visiting emigrants from the United States are called, but are mostly critical of them; often my wife and I have been asked on first meeting an Irish person whether we are Irish-Americans or "real Americans," and when we have admitted to being the latter we have been well received. Conversely, we have seen Yanks shunned on revealing their pedigree. They are accused of "lording it over" their Irish kin and friends.

Formal Social Control

Anthropologists customarily classify social control systems as formal and informal. Formal systems are governments whose controls are based on physical violence or its threat—physical punishment, ostracism, banishment, and extermination; while informal systems include sanctions of a religious or economic nature and those exercised by primary groups—gossip, ridicule, persuasion, and opprobrium. Controls of a negative nature are buttressed by positive rewards, such as services provided by a government or the feeling of security gained from primary group approval. It is not the formal system of local and national governments which exerts the most control over the behavior of Inis Beag islanders, but rather the church whose clerical representatives impose supernatural sanctions more potent than the threat of extermination. Indeed, because of the marked theocratic tendencies of the church in the Republic, and the all-powerful political role played by the clergy in Inis Beag, it is tempting to label the church a formal agency of social control. The island certainly comprises a primary group in the sociological sense, with its diminutive size and population, and the sanctions imposed by the folk on one another sometimes rival in effectiveness those of the parish priest and curate.

The widespread peasant trait of dependence together with hostility toward government is most pronounced in Inis Beag. Aid in a variety of forms constantly is sought and even expected as an obligation, or "right," of the government by the islanders (especially since nativism engendered by the Gaelic Revival has made Inis Beag "the darling of the Gaeltacht," to quote a Dublin scholar who is a bitter foe of the language movement), but they are either apathetic or antagonistic toward the local and central governments. When asked to account for their anti-government sentiment, the folk of Inis Beag cite most often the commonplace nepotism and corruption practiced by functionaries, the slight differences between the platforms of the major Irish parties—Fianna Fail and Fine Gael, the promises made by politicians which seldom are kept when they achieve office, the misapplication of programs once implemented, the inadequacy of government services, the burden of increasing taxation and inflation, and "foolish" government projects in Inis Beag, more often than not instituted without consulting the islanders.

Today, the folk seldom pay heed to election promises, but once their votes were commanded by politicians who put forth grandiose plans for the betterment of local conditions—such as lengthening the present jetty or constructing another to accommodate the steamer, and connecting the fresh water lake with the sea to form a sheltered harbor for trawlers—which never were realized. Popular subjects of conversation are the shortcomings of the postal, medical, transport, and other services, and the steady increase of taxes—on stout and tobacco in particular —and the price of imported turf. Among the government projects criticized by the islanders are seaweed drying structures and lime kilns which seldom or never have been used, road improvements made where they were not needed and not made where they were needed, and the new school and jetty whose sites were misplaced by civil servants who failed to seek local advice as to the vagaries of wind and tide. The school is in danger of becoming inundated with sand from the common land, and is near the strand where activities distract the attention of the pupils; and the pier is not located in the most protected position that the coastline affords. Anti-government feeling is but a part of a much broader anti-authority configuration, which extends to the clergy, to high status folk, and even to parent-child and sibling relationships within the family. It has been for many centuries a component of Irish basic personality structure and has had momentous repercussions on the course of Irish history.

The political apathy of the islanders is revealed in their voting behavior and their knowledge of political figures and issues. Election of councillors to the county council takes place every two years, and election of members to the Dail (the lower House of Parliament) every five. Candidates for the Dail occasionally visit Inis Beag to campaign briefly, but candidates for the county council seldom do because of the lack of interest shown in local elections and the small number of voters. In the last local election, approximately 60 of 194 eligible voters cast ballots, while the previous national election attracted slightly less than 100 voters. Two clerks from the island supervise the voting, which takes place in the school between nine o'clock in the morning and nine at night, five days before the rest of the nation votes. No more than a handful of the people are politically aware and committed enough to campaign actively among their fellows. Political discussions animate the island a week or two before an election, but most of the people are poorly informed about the records and platforms of candidates and parties. Estimates vary as to the strength of the parties in Inis Beag; Fianna Fail receives anywhere from 50 to 90 percent of the votes cast, according to various respondents, whereas Fine Gael receives most of the rest with Labour a very weak third. The tendency among the folk is to vote party rather than politician, although the fortunes of Fianna Fail have depended largely on the popularity of aging President Eamon de Valera; "Dev" is regarded as "cute," not to be trusted, and vacillatory, but his fame outside of Ireland, which reflects to the credit of the nation, is the all important criterion of judgment among the local electorate. Some islanders have urged voters to interest themselves more in the local than national elections, arguing that many services and subsidies are provided by the county council, and its elected representatives can be "supervised" more closely than their Dail counterparts.

The local and national governments impinge on the lives of the folk most importantly through the many services and subsidies which are provided by agencies of the two bodies and implemented by visiting or locally appointed or hired functionaries. I have made reference already to certain government commitments: the language program and knitting industry, both underwritten by Gaeltacht Eireann, several of the agricultural measures supervised by Department of Agriculture representatives, the life saving company maintained by the Coast Life Saving Service, maintenance tasks performed by island men hired by the Irish Lights Service, and the post office and national school. Mention also should be made of the doctor stationed in a neighboring island, the local agent of the Irish Transport System who oversees the unloading and loading of cargo shipped on the steamer, and the islander who serves in three capacities as county council agent, supervisor of road improvements under the Special Employment Schemes Office, and bailiff. As bailiff, he signs official forms for the folk, can take an offender into custody and set bail, and must sign a warrant before the police can make an arrest in Inis Beag.

There are no police, called *gardai* and "guards," in the island, but three, including a sergeant, are posted in a nearby island and visit Inis Beag at least once a month. Crime is virtually unknown among the folk, the few cases on record being for assault and battery and destruction of property; most cases are civil ones, involving property ownership and inheritance, and are tried intermittently by a visiting magistrate. The guards are subjected to frequent criticism and derision, especially when they come to the island dressed in plain-clothes to search for unlicensed dogs, or when they discover a still on the mainland and arrest the "poor creatures" who were manufacturing "poteen" (illicit whiskey). They sometimes are called "peelers" in reference, a derogatory term assigned to their predecessors, the Royal Irish Constabulary, founded by Sir Robert Peel. (The Irish chose his surname to immortalize and the English his Christian name—"bobbie.") Seven verses of my ballad satirize the much resented role of the police during the aftermath of the shipwreck. The absence of guards in Inis Beag means that the pubs can stay open after legal hours, sometimes until two or three o'clock in the morning; and in the island where the police are stationed, one must enter the pubs after hours, if permitted, by the back door and drink sitting on the floor.

The *Guide to the Social Services*, published by the Dublin Stationary Office in 1959, lists under 76 headings the multitudinous services and subsidies provided the Irish people by local and central governments. Among the most important to Inis Beag folk are: Widow's Pension, Old Age Pension (called "the old age"), Unemployment Assistance (know as "the dole"), Children's Allowances, General Medical Services, General Institutional and Specialist Services, Mental Treatment, Disabled Persons Maintenance Allowances, Maternity and Infant Services, Free School Books in National Schools, Employment and Special Emergency Schemes (which include road improvement), Agricultural Education, Schemes of Agricultural Development, Gaeltacht Eireann Schemes (which include housing and language subsidies), Private Housing Grants and Loans, Local Authority Housing, and Land Commission Housing. Most of these programs are handled by civil servants who visit Inis Beag from a nearby island or the mainland, and at any time during the year there is usually at least one government agent conducting his business in the island. The services and subsidies are welcomed by the folk even though seldom considered adequate, and only one arouses bitter antagonism: elders dislike the law which requires them to will their land at age 70 before they can go on the old age, as well as the probing of functionaries who request personal information of potential old age pensioners, especially information about remittance monies which might disqualify the applicants. Almost all of the islanders are on the dole, and few express outwardly embarrassment or shame as regards the fact —"The government has a right to give us the dole."

Informal Social Control

The informal social control system of Inis Beag comprises the parish priest and curate, the headmaster of the school—chosen and strictly regulated by the parish priest, and a "king." The position of king is not hereditary and not supported by a majority of the population as in some other Irish islands, but is self-assumed and based on a number of factors to be considered shortly. Not only is king strictly a term of reference, but it is employed by the folk only when they are most critical of his actions; it also is used by certain outsiders who are frequent visitors to Inis Beag and are aware of the power structure there, but always out of earshot of the islanders.

The role of the church in Irish history has been well documented, albeit often in a biased manner because of the prejudices of certain historians, but its role in shaping Irish culture and personality has been little examined. Irish social scientists either have been oblivious to it because of being Catholics themselves, or have been fearful of the political and religious consequences were they to pursue and publish the "truth;" foreign scientists, on the other hand, have shown little interest in Ireland, or have suppressed their data on religious influences in order to be able to return there to do further research.

Whereas in developing countries anthropologists are being restricted increasingly by elitists sensitive to the primitive conditions in their nations which are being studied and publicized by scientists, in Ireland similar reactions of nativists, including those who are in the government, are compounded by those of the church. The resistance of the church to objective scrutiny in large measure explains the absence of ethnology—with its emphasis on such values as empiricism, naturalism, relativism, and pluralism—as a discipline in the national universities. Irish scholars have tended to stress economic and other monistic causes (especially climate, race, English oppression, the famine, and loss of the Irish tongue) in their analyses of culture and personality phenomena. I have talked with Irish scientists about religious forces as aspects of particular phenomena, and have been told that to acknowledge certain of these in print would be to commit job suicide. When I have discussed with them my own conclusions about factors accounting for such conditions in Inis Beag as celibacy, late marriage, personality disorders, and emigration, and have cited religious causes as among the most significant ones, my listeners have agreed tacitly and changed the subject, or have remained silent. Irish scientists visiting the United States, I might add, usually endorse my views but often ask not to be quoted abroad or in print. Religious causes are, in fact, so important and pervasive that one runs the risk of being declared a "religious determinist" if he deals objectively with his materials.

The bishop and the parish priest in theory direct the actions of the curate in Inis Beag, but it is believed by the folk that their control over him in reality is only nominal, and that he often is able to make and carry out major decisions affecting the welfare of the islanders without consulting his superiors. His supposed freedom of action is reflected in the commonly voiced complaint that if word of his secular "excesses" were to reach the bishop, he would be reprimanded or replaced. However, some say that his policies are known and secretly approved of by his superiors. It is rumored that I was responsible for the replacement of a curate by complaining of his opposition to my research and certain of his excesses to mainlanders who had the "ear of the bishop."

The folk are devoutly Catholic, despite the fact that they are extremely critical of their priests and retain and reinterpret pagan religious forms. They are proud of their strength of belief, with its attendant morality, and of the sanctity of "Inis Beag of the Saints," and they look to the curate for spiritual comfort, as well as political guidance in several spheres, and are uncomfortable in his absence. His presence, it is believed, provides supernatural protection for the island, while his absence invites possible anti-social behavior, and harm to the soul of one who dies suddenly and is deprived of Extreme Unction at his deathbed. The compensatory rite performed later for the deceased who has been interred while the curate was away is thought to be less efficacious in shortening the stay of the soul in Purgatory.

In the past, the amount of social control exerted by clerics has varied; a few have been concerned mostly with fulfilling their religious duties, but the greater number have attempted in a variety of ways to regulate the lives of the islanders —to restrict such activities as visiting, gossiping, courting, dancing, and drinking spirits. The curates have tried, in general, to maintain the indigenous culture, especially the Gaelic tongue, and to discourage change, halt emigration, maintain the moral standards of the folk, and limit anti-social behavior. I have heard both islanders and curates defend the *status quo* in Inis Beag, including its poverty, by asserting that, "This life is of no importance, and its suffering must be borne for the glory of Heaven to come." In the absence of local police, curates sometimes have performed the functions of *gardaí*, and since 1960 have combatted a growing rash of juvenile delinquency, which has included, among other misdeeds, the destruction of property outside of homes in which parties are held, petty theft, and molestation of girls from the mainland who visit during the summer.

The techniques of social control utilized by curates are many and mostly negative; they include weekly sermons, lectures to students in the school, talks with individuals who need guidance or reprimand, the use of informers (a word so detested in Ireland that I have substituted respondent for informant in this book) and confessions, the allocation of indulgences, and, in extreme cases, the refusal of sacraments and the placing of curses. It is difficult to overestimate the degree of fear of the clergy and anti-clericalism which have been inculcated among the folk by the more immoderate measures employed by priests during the last century. Sermons deal both with spiritual messages based on the scriptures and church pronouncements, and with instruction and censure directed toward past or anticipated actions of the islanders in concert or of particular persons. Talks with individuals may take place in their or the curate's home, and often result from information received by the priest from informers or the confessional. The informers, it is said, are usually the housekeeper of the curate and her family, and children who are intimidated by the priest to reveal talk and behavior of their parents and others; however, certain folk are known to bear tales to the clergy and are shunned for this reason. Well aware of the power that the confessional gives the priest over their lives, islanders are outspoken in its condemnation, and many will not confess particular sins, especially those of a sexual nature, to a curate known to assign severe penances and to carry matters beyond the confessional.

The awarding of indulgences represents a positive social control method and has been used frequently, I was told, to obtain needed monetary contributions and services from the folk. Although the priest cannot excommunicate a recalcitrant parishioner, he can achieve the same objective by forbidding confession and absolution and the other sacraments to him, and the islanders report its threat and use as a sanction on several occasions in the past. Even more feared is the "priest's curse," which in Co. Clare ". . . can bring ruin upon a prosperous house; can turn an unbeliver's head upon his shoulders; strike blindness . . ." (Arensberg 1937:28).

In Inis Beag, it is called "reading the Gospel (or Bible) at," and can bring illness or death and ultimate damnation within a prescribed time; the folk reason that if a cleric can cure with prayer, he also can cause illness and death by its use.

One other control technique of the clergy must be mentioned—that of influencing civil servants to implement their wishes. One case among many that I recorded, based partly on rumor, will serve as an example of its potency. A middle-aged, unmarried man who anticipated inheriting land discovered that his widowed mother, with the advice of the curate and unknown to himself until the last moment, had "signed it over" to his younger brother who wished to marry. In his rage, the betrayed man threatened the priest who came to pacify him, and the following day he was removed to a mental institution. The folk accuse the curate of "forcing" the doctor to commit their neighbor, on the pretext that on occasion he acted "strangely" and held himself aloof from many of his fellows. Six months later he was released from the hospital as normal—according to Irish law which states that a patient under observation cannot be institutionalized for more than that period if declared sane—and he emigrated to England. Whether or not the curate prevailed on the doctor can never be known, but the islanders believe that he did and can cite equally extreme cases involving other priests and funtionaries. The curate in question soon afterward was committed to the "mad-house" himself, which was, according to the folk, a form of divine punishment.

Anti-clerical sentiment is strong in Inis Beag, although it is seldom manifested in acts of overt resistance to the will of the curate. An outsider must be careful not to voice a like sentiment, or, for that matter, evince agreement with diatribes directed against the clergy by islanders with whom he is conversing, or he will evoke a spirited defense of the church and be accused of anti-clericalism— or worse. The response of the folk reveals the deeply rooted ambivalence that they feel toward the church: how they revere its doctrines yet resent many actions of its representatives. An outspoken elder told me of his views concerning the church, which are shared by most of his less "bold" comrades: "The trouble with Ireland is the priests. They took over after the famine, when the population had halved and their number had quadrupled, and broke our spirit by preaching damnation and the sinfulness of sex. We came to depend on them instead of ourselves, and today they live off us but are strangers in our midst. They should be concerned only with the salvation of our immortal souls. Birds know more about God and his wishes for man than they do. The reason that we flee the country is to escape their control and the dull life they have created."

Criticisms of past and present curates are so numerous that only the most repeated ones, which arouse the most resentment and anger when aired, can be taken up. There is a constant plea for older priests to be assigned to Inis Beag— men who have experienced life elsewhere in Ireland and abroad and know its countless facets, and who have developed compassion for the human condition— rather than the "young, pink-cheeked Maynooth Seminary graduates" who often are assigned. As well as being youthful and naive, the folk feel that too many priests have acted aloof and supercilious, have been unhappy with their Inis Beag post, and have marked time waiting for their tenure to end. Their lack of commitment has meant, it is believed, frequent shirking of their duties toward the folk. Chronic negligence in the care of chapel and school is regarded as a symptom of the indifference of the clerics (or laziness, according to some), as is their seeming unwillingness to provide leadership at crucial times. The intrusion of the clergy into spheres of island life where their influence is unwarranted, according to local opinion, and their methods of controlling behavior give rise to the greatest amount of criticism, but need not be considered further at this juncture. As elsewhere in Ireland, and a source of countless humorous anecdotes and jokes, the style of life of many priests contributes to anti-clericalism. The comfort of the curates' home (particularly the new one erected since 1960, by one islander called "the house indulgences built"), their menu, their offering of tobacco and whiskey to guests, their visits to mainland, Continent, and even America, are all discussed frequently and resentfully by the folk.

Linked with the much criticized life style of clerics are the many demands made on the islanders for monetary contributions. It is felt that the diocese is wealthy enough to support the parish priest and his curates and need not "keep the people poor" by forcing them to donate money and services without charge for their upkeep. In addition to regular offerings on Sunday, the people are called on to proffer more substantial sums at Christmas, Easter, and on several other occasions during the year. My wife and I made donations at Christmas and Easter despite the urging of many not to do so—"You are hated by the priests, so why give them money?" The names of contributors and their donations are announced from the pulpit or posted in the chapel. This practice is another control technique of sorts and infuriates many of the folk.

Other major sources of antagonism toward the clergy are their poor Gaelic and the fact that they urge the people to speak only Irish yet converse among themselves in English; their criticism of valued island customs, particularly of pagan reinterpretations; their conservatism and resistance to change, which results in the folk being ill prepared to emigrate when they must; their susceptibility to influence by the king, especially those who are newly graduated and are uncertain of themselves and their role; and their demands on canoe crews which must row them back and forth to Inis Thiar and other islands, often in dangerous weather. A conception of what the curate "ought to be like" was voiced by a pious but troubled woman: "He should be humble, not have money when so many poor are about, not treat the people as inferior, and not be afraid to work hard."

It is difficult to ascertain today whether the headmaster or the king should be accorded the dominant position, after the curate, in the informal social control system of Inis Beag; for in recent years, the power and prestige of the former have been waxing and those of the latter waning. Headmasters were formerly older men with families whose tenure was long, who were much involved in local affairs and worked closely with the curate, who were politically active and backed candidates and tried to influence island voters, and who maintained social distance although considered "one of the people." For their teaching and other services, they were provided with food, given *curach* transportation without charge, and afforded other amenities by the folk. The house that they and their families occupied until recently is located in Castle Village, near both the old and new schools, and was owned by the diocese. Headmasters now are younger and often single, and are more independent of the curate (One in recent years quit his post, it is held, because he chafed at restrictions imposed on him by the priest.); also, they are apolitical and participate less in the gamut of local affairs. The prestige of the headmaster derives from his having been selected by the parish priest who supports his actions, his status as a "scholar," and the discipline that he exerts in the school with its vestigial effects on those who have graduated. Few islanders will openly contest his decisions in school and in civic matters.

The important nonacademic tasks performed by the headmaster are sign-ing official forms—a duty that he shares with the bailiff, drawing up and witnessing the signing of wills, writing letters for the islanders, especially those directed to the county council and departments of the central government, and giving advice on such matters as the advisability of emigrating and of matrimonial matches. Like the curates, the headmasters seldom have tried to direct community projects and social affairs, other than dances and inter-island competitions. The present headmaster considers himself atypical in many respects, in that he is youthful, has exceptional skill in playing the accordion, likes companionship and the festivities of party and pub, and has rapport with older boys and young men with whom he associates more than did his predecessors; as a result, he is the prime mover in social events—organizing dances and donating his musical talent. Older islanders often find him aloof and will apologize for "taking his time" when seeking favors of him.

Parents have little contact with the headmaster as regards the education of their children, and, although permitted and sometimes urged to do so, they seldom visit the school. They will consult with him about such matters as health problems of their children, but not about educational policies; nor do they complain to him of his role as pedagogue—"What the teacher does is right." Because of the severity of his discipline, and that of the other two teachers, and the fear that it arouses in his pupils, parents use him as a threat in disciplining their children at home. This is a distinction that he shares with the nurse and her hypodermic needle and me with my large size and robust manner; being the ominous *Fear an Stáisiún* ("Man of the Station," because my wife and I rented for a time an apartment in the coast guard station) made it difficult for me to obtain young people as respondents until many months had passed. As a result of the rigid discipline exerted in the school, maintained by actions which include even whipping and priestly impreca-tion, a degree of orderliness, quietness, and attentiveness on the part of the students is achieved which would arouse incredulity among American teachers and parents unless witnessed. Discipline in the school merely reflects that in the home, and a favorite pastime of Irish living in the vicinity of Shannon Airport is to observe the interaction of American parents and their usually obstreperous offspring in the transient room there.

Whereas the headmaster attracts the least amount of anti-authority senti-ment of any other figure who regulates to a marked degree the lives of the folk, the king attracts the most. The latter is the senior of the two publicans, in age and role, whose home in Low Village accommodates guests as well as the shop and pub. Information concerning him was as difficult to come by as that concerning curates whom I knew, in that he resented my presence and refused to cooperate with me in my research; thus, I am forced to depend on data about his career provided me by his neighbors. It is hard to disentangle fact from hearsay in these materials, for he arouses extremes of feeling among islanders which can prompt distortions of information. I was told by several respondents—bitter foes of the king—that he conceives of himself as the moral guardian of the folk "who knows what is best for them;" he believes them to possess a childlike mentality and outlook on the world which necessitate his guidance (In talking with these respondents, who referred to the king as "the little priest," I was reminded of interviews in Africa seven years earlier concerning particular British colonial administrators, who conceived of their relationship with the Nigerians in like manner.).

A personable man of great charm, the king has a measure of charisma which commands deference and respect, and it is said that had he chosen to become a priest or businessman on the mainland, he would now be a bishop or captain of industry. His business acumen is acclaimed, and many have become his customers because they believe him to be more "clever" than city merchants and well able to deal with them to the advantage of the islanders. The sources of his power are many. He began his career as a shopkeeper in the 1920s, with money provided him by a brother living in the United States (or, as claimed by some, with the insurance money that he received as a beneficiary when his brother was killed while serving in the armed forces of this country). Two brothers older than himself—the eldest the landholder—live in Inis Beag with large families, and he has their support and that of his many other kin. He gained a large following during the depression years of the 1930s by extending credit to customers for months without charging interest; many folk still show gratitude for this gesture by buying only from him and by acquiescing to many of his wishes, although covertly they may resent being in his debt and under his influence. He is a friend of priests, politicians, and civil servants, who usually reside in his guest house when visiting Inis Beag, and he is a political activist in behalf of "Dev" and Fianna Fail. Another source of his power is the fact that he cashes most of the checks and changes most of the foreign currency received by the islanders, and thus knows of sources and amounts of income; it is feared that he might inform government officials of remittances and as a result jeopardize the old age and dole of any who earn his displeasure.

The king is most criticized for his "great riches," which arouse envy and jealousy in his neighbors. From time to time, rumors as to the amount of money deposited to his account in a mainland bank pass around Inis Beag, and arouse discussion of the bill of particulars against him. His involvement in the salvaging of the cargo of the grounded freighter brought to the surface all of the hostility toward him felt by the folk. He is supposed to have pooled his resources with several businessmen "from the city" to purchase the most valuable items of the cargo for resale at a "vast profit;" to safeguard these items until they could be salvaged and shipped off on the steamer, he consorted with owners of the steamship company, customs officials, the guards, and even the curate to prevent the islanders ("who only saved the lives of the crew") from observing the law of wrack and thereby reducing his profit. It is held that he persuaded the curate to deliver sermons denouncing the "looting" of the ship as sinful, and he allowed his partners to come to Inis Beag to confer with him, knowing that they were ill with influenza, which resulted in a serious outbreak of the disease shortly afterward. A fire which broke out in a storage room next to the house of the king some months after the shipwreck was viewed by irate islanders as divine retribution for his "greed and selfishness."

In Ireland, the term "gombeen" is used to demean the usurious shopkeeper, but this word is directed against the king only by those who most dislike him, and then to connote what they consider a combination of piety and avarice in his behavior rather than his economic practices. His role as moral guardian, with frequent instruction and reprimand as to manners and misdemeanors to men in the pub and children visiting the shop, is deeply resented by many. He does not care to have women make purchases in the shop, where they can observe men drinking and be observed in turn, ostensibly on moral grounds; he urges that children do the marketing instead, not for the convenience of their mothers, it is said, but because he can overcharge and short-change them more easily. To dissuade women from shopping, he reads out their lists and talks with them about family affairs in a loud whisper, so that they have no privacy. The men complain not only of his alleged practice of overcharging and short-changing them late at night when the pub is overcrowded with "light headed" drinkers, but also of his criticizing their actions in public, his frequent closing of the pub before midnight, and his refusal to serve those whom he feels have "taken too much" or those about to attend a party where more drinks will be proffered them.

Supporters of Fine Gael and Labour, among others, object to the manner in which the king curries the favor of Fianna Fail representatives and campaigns for the party. He is accused of using illegal tactics, such as haranguing voters outside of the school as they enter to cast their ballots, in his endeavor to keep Fianna Fail in power. A more serious charge related to this one is his opposition to change in Inis Beag which might benefit the population as a whole, an opposition which explains his support of political party and church—both conservative forces. It is asserted that, just as the government wants to preserve the Gaelic language and supposed Celtic virtues of the folk and the church their strength of belief and morality and thus underwrite the *status quo*, the senior publican wants no changes which might threaten his economic position and control over the lives of the islanders. To this end, he is thought to use his influence with priests and politicians who are in a position to modify local conditions.

Absent from Inis Beag is the evening *cuaird* of old men, which plays such a decisive role in the political and social life of villages on the mainland. It is a clique of visitors who usually convene at a particular home, called the "old men's house," to formulate local policies.

> Much of the community's relation to the outer world is debated here and determined by the old men's agreement.... It is here that petitions for roads, for relief work in winter, for extension of agricultural prize schemes, and all of the "political" business of the county council and its committees originates on the side of the local community. It is here too that the community reaches its unanimity in party voting.... Here it is too that the community makes its appraisal of its own members and those with whom it is in contact. And that appraisal tells quite heavily in the behavior the community will adopt toward the person or

> conditions appraised.... The community regulates its internal affairs through
> the *cuaird* as well. It is here public opinion is formulated. There is nothing formal
> about the decisions made upon the incidents arising from day to day. The local
> community has no implement with which to enforce its will. But it has the power
> of gossip and ... boycott (Arensberg and Kimball 1940:190–191).

Decisions of this sort and their sanctions in Inis Beag rest largely in the hands of
government officials and the priest, headmaster, and king.

Many folk long have believed that the island needs a council with representatives from each of the four villages serving on it, to foster cooperation and
to formulate policies which bear on the welfare of all. After independence in
1922, a move was made to form such a council, but the civil war interrupted the
process; since that time, according to the islanders, the opposition of curates and
king, none of whom have wanted their vested interests threatened, has succeeded
in blocking the formation of such a body. Other forces at work, however, are the
lassitude and ambivalence toward authority of the people, and their dislike and
jealousy of one another. They complain of the lack of leadership, or of the "wrong"
kind of leadership, as in the case of the priest and king; but they are unable or
unwilling to expend the energy needed to get themselves organized and "pull
together" for the common good. Often those who advocate the formation of a
council will, in the next breath, express their dislike or distrust of its potential
members, or a desire to remain independent of its collective will should it run
contrary to their own. A vacationing emigrant who said, "We have no sense of
civic pride and responsibility but think only of ourselves.", assessed the situation
accurately.

Among the traits attributed to Inis Beag folk by nativists and primitivists
are self-reliance, independence, and individualism. But the self-reliance of the
islanders has become undermined increasingly since 1891 by a benevolent government; their independence is severely curtailed by restrictions imposed on them
by curate, headmaster, king, and their fellows; and their individualism is a figment
of literary imagination disguising a strict conformism. Inis Beag as much as any
community is characterized by gossip, ridicule, and opprobrium, which gain their
effectiveness as social control mechanisms from the deep concern of the folk with
"saving face," and which serve to limit freedom of action and behavioral idio-
syncrasy. When asked to rank the major deficiencies of island life, the people
almost without exception place the prevalence of malicious gossiping, along with
poverty and the intrusion of the clergy into secular affairs, at the head of their list.

No matter how much the islanders detest gossiping when they are its
victims, they nevertheless welcome every opportunity to engage in it. News of an
event passes quickly by word of mouth from Low to Terrace Villages, and variations in the description of the event are usually numerous due to the distortions of
rumor. In order to circumvent gossip, parties are organized at the last moment and
invitations issued by small boys moving quietly from door to door in the night;
persons will leave the island—sometimes to emigrate, visit the hospital with a
serious illness, or enter an order—without previous announcement, running from
their homes to the strand to board the last canoes for the steamer; and mail is
posted just prior to the arrival of the steamer and picked up immediately after it

is carried to the post office, for fear that the postmaster will open letters and talk publicly of their contents (or take money from them). It is customary for boys and young men to hide themselves in the darkness or behind fences in order to over-hear conversations of passersby, or witness their misbehavior, which can be re-ported; this compels folk who move about after dark to conceal their faces and talk in whispers or low tones. When a person hidden in the darkness is accosted sud-denly, he will vault a fence, run away, or crouch down and hide his face or draw a raincoat over his head and shoulders to avoid being recognized. Most social events and visiting take place after sundown, so that movements from one house to another will be unobserved.

Deviant behavior once learned of assures its perpetrators of becoming the focus of gossip and ridicule. But ridicule seldom is voiced in the presence of the victim; rather, he or she is told of it by relatives and acquaintances who have witnessed or, more commonly, been told of it by others. My ballad not only took advantage of the ubiquity of rumor, but its composition, aided and abetted by two dozen respondents, enabled me to discover the existence of a seldom revealed tradition of satirical balladry, common to the Irish, which has singled out for opprobrium many folk in the past. During three summer visits to Inis Beag following 1960, my wife and I were able to witness the singing of my song pub-licly. We learned that it, as others of its genre, is sung only before small gatherings, and whether or not it (or certain of its verses) is sung and by whom depends on the makeup of the assembled group. Since ridicule is almost never expressed in the presence of its victim or his kin or close friends, we were able to gain informa-tion about kinship relations and factionalism by noting the juxtaposition of balladiers and audiences and which verses were sung.

Courtship and Marriage

Marriages are fewer and are entered into later in Ireland than in any other Western country. In 1951, approximately one-third of the men and one-quarter of the women in Ireland between the ages of 55 and 64 years had never married, while two-thirds of the men and two-fifths of the women between 25 and 34 years of age were single. Celibacy and age of marriage figures for Inis Beag approximate those for the rest of peasant Ireland. In a population of 350 persons, 116 are married; 13 are widows; 3 are widowers; and 33 males over 23 years of age and 21 females over 17 are single. Since marriage occurs between the ages of 24 and 45 years for men and 18 and 32 for women, based on statistics extending back to 1911, only 18 men and 9 women (excluding 3 women who, because of physical disabilities, probably never will marry) are eligible for marriage. Not only are 34.4 percent of the males bachelors and 22.6 percent of the females spinsters, but the average marriage age for men in the period 1951 to 1960 was 35.5 years and for women 24.8 (compared to an average for rural Ireland of 34.7 years for men and 28.7 for women in 1946). The age span between spouses married during the past half-century ranges from the husband being 21 years older than his wife to 4 years younger, but the average age span has been between 8 and 12 years for each of the five decades. The number of marriages per decade has been declining steadily, and between 1951 and 1960 there were only nine marriages between folk who remained in the island—and since then but five.

The prevalence of celibacy and late marriage is a matter of grave concern to the people. My analysis of these phenomena reveals over 20 contributing factors, of which I will consider only the most important—and these briefly, since most of them will be addressed further within the contexts of the family, personality, and emigration. The one most often voiced by the islanders is the emigration of girls in increasing numbers at younger ages; of the nine girls eligible for marriage, only one is older than 25 years, and several are contemplating emigration. The folk are much less prone to talk of the single estate and late marriage than they are of emigration, which share many of the same causes, and they appear to know fewer of the causes of the former and are less willing to assign relative weights when assessing them. The cause of all three conditions most often cited by both writers and social scientists is the system of inheritance, whereby land cannot be sub-divided but is passed on to one son who must wait to marry until his father dies or is willing (or forced) to pass on the land, and his siblings have married or emigrated. By this time, the son is usually middle-aged and cautious in making his choice of a spouse. Most fathers in Inis Beag are loath to surrender their property, and with it control of the family, to sons wishing to marry, and some even will postpone receiving the old age in order to maintain their status position past the age of 70 years. A father who does not choose a successor among several sons until late in his life—which is a common occurrence—can retard their marriages if they choose to "wait it out." Equally loath to disturb the family *status quo* is the mother, who fears not only the loss of her commanding position in the household, but the loss of her son's affection to an incoming daughter-in-law. The man who wishes to marry and is prevented from doing so by domineering and jealous parents is the subject of gossip, and his plight is regarded as a "shame."

Since late marriage has been a persistent phenomenon in Ireland since the great famine, it has become institutionalized and serves as an expectation for young people. That the folk are aware of this cause is attested by their frequent advice to offspring that they postpone marriage to conform to island tradition. This advice invariably is buttressed by a rationale of males not having enough "sense" to marry until they approach the age of 40 years. Reflected in the rationale is the system of male age grading conceptualized in Inis Beag: a man is a "boy" or "lad" until 40 years of age, an adult until 60 years, middle-aged until 80, and old-aged after that (exhilarating to the American anthropologist who comes from a society obsessed with the "cult of youth"). Another rationale for late marriage often heard in Inis Beag is the impossibility of divorce in Catholic Ireland, which demands that the choice of a spouse be well considered. It appears that this argument is usually used to explain late marriage when other factors are in fact responsible—certainly when "considering" covers two or more decades.

Two closely linked causes of celibacy and late marriage seldom broached in Inis Beag are male solidarity and the unwillingness of many men to accept the re-sponsibilities of marriage, particularly its sexual responsibilities. Marriage is looked on with trepidation, or at least as something less than desirable. The marriageable man in his late twenties and thirties is usually sexually repressed to an unbelieveable degree, has been dominated by parents who have allowed him to take on few major responsibilities, has a mother who acts as a wife surrogate in all but the sexual sphere (at least consciously), has established a routinized existence, and has male companions for whom he feels affection and with whom he shares numerous work and recreational activities. Some men who have been promised or willed land, and who have consenting parents and brides-to-be, will balk at a match because they are "too happy with the lads," and, if persuaded to marry, they will attempt to retain as much of their bachelor role as possible within marriage—"The men run with the boys before marriage and carry on the same afterward." Several bachelors and spinsters almost have married several times in succession, only to find the sexual commitment on each occasion too difficult to make at the last moment.

Before the coming of a permanent priest to Inis Beag, it is asserted that young people contemplating marriage were able to "keep company" frequently and openly before the union was arranged, and that some pairings were "love matches." But since then—with the separation of the sexes from late infancy on, the ubiquity of gossip and opprobrium, and the actions of priests—courting almost has disappeared, and it is not uncommon for a couple awaiting their wedding to have little personal knowledge of one another. Contact on the island between the sexes today is limited to meetings at the few parties which take place, at the occasional summer dances, or *céilí*, held on a large flagging near the school, and sometimes "at the well" or "walking to the cow" during daylight hours. Two generations ago, private Sunday afternoon strolls afforded young men and women the opportunity of coming to know one another well, but these "rambles" about the island are done now only by couples of the same sex—one of the several manifestations of institutionalized friendship. Choice once again seems to be intruding into matchmaking, however, with the increasing demands of acculturated youths for marriage with "love."

Matches are the end product either of secret bargaining between the families involved which can extend for weeks, or of the impetuous act of a man who—goaded by companions or by stout, or both—will visit the home of his "chosen" after dark to negotiate, accompanied by a kinsman or close friend. The bargain, once made, is sealed by the male participants with the emptying of a bottle of whiskey brought by the prospective groom, after which a boy or young man of the household is sent out—often after midnight—to summon relatives and acquaintances for a night long party, known as the *cleamhnas* (the word for matchmaking in Gaelic). Sometimes this party is followed by as many as three more on consecutive nights, the expense for which is borne by the family of the bride-to-be. When the bargaining is protracted, it usually is done during the 12 days of Christmas or the final fortnight of Lent, and the match is announced soon after Epiphany or Easter. Hearsay concerning possible matches abounds at these times, but each year "most rumors are dry," unless, of course, "with a lot of drinking and urging a man might decide to take the plunge." It was customary in the past for the wedding to take place four days after the *cleamhnas*, but now the service must wait from one to three weeks until the genealogies of the families of the bride and groom are examined by the parish priest to determine their degree of consanguinity.

Numerous factors are weighed by the representatives of the future spouses before a match is consummated. Uppermost in the minds of the relatives of the man is the size of the dowry that the woman will bring to the marriage. In the decade 1951 to 1960, the average dowry was 50 to 60 pounds, but at least one reached 100 pounds. This sum now is used to finance the wedding party, but once it went to provide the passage and "settling in" money for an emigrating sibling, to furnish the dowry for a daughter, or to make life more comfortable for the aging parents. Land and capital (and other status attributes soon to be discussed) possessed by the father or widowed mother of the man are the focal concern of the woman's relatives during matchmaking. Among the factors which enter into the deliberations of both bargaining parties are: the presence in either family line of mental illness or other afflictions which can stigmatize, the economic skills and industriousness of the potential spouses, the number of cognates (relatives on all sides of ego limited only by degree of kinship) which compose the two kin-groups and their propensity to assist and defend (and not to engage in disputes), and the mutual attraction of body and personality of the future spouses. The folk believe that young persons approaching marriage "should have known each other for a long spell" and that "the two should be alike"—as to family position, education, and temperament. It is common for a woman to choose not to marry a man to whom she may be attracted because his mother is overly jealous and domineering, or there are "too many old people in the house."

Most weddings take place on Tuesday during the hour before noon, at the direction of the curate, but at one time they were conducted between four and five o'clock in the afternoon, so that the guests could hurry back to the groom's house "to make a night of it;" the morning ceremony means that festivities commence in mid-afternoon and the party often is "stale by nightfall." Each family invites its circle of relatives and friends who congregate at the respective domiciles in the morning, where the men are served whiskey. The groom's entourage then accompanies him to the house of the bride, and another "round" is proffered them before the procession is formed for the journey to the chapel and back. Three men lead the column at some distance from the bride and groom, to ward off those with the evil eye or any other malignant forces which might threaten the couple. Close behind the bride and groom are the "best man" and "maid of honor," followed in order by the two fathers, male guests in a group, and at the end female guests; the two mothers do not attend the wedding, nor does the bride's mother participate in the matchmaking or allow her daughter to return home until a month following the nuptials (Formerly, she did not enter her daughter's house until a grandchild was born.).

Grooms long have worn mainland attire for the ceremony, but only in 1960 did the first bride do so. Before then, the woman wore a new blue petticoat, accouterments purchased in shops at a nearby mainland port, and a shawl for the first time, draped over the shoulders. Her hair had remained uncut until this day, and she and the groom wore borrowed items of clothing—she usually the shawl and he a coat or tie—to bring luck to their marriage. During the nuptial service, the man not only places a ring on the finger of his bride, but gives her seven shillings with which to buy later a holy picture, or some other object of her choosing. The kiss of the newly united pair, which in most of the Western world terminates the marriage ceremony, is lacking in Inis Beag, and after leaving the chapel the couple stand for some time in the yard to receive congratulations from guests and others who have attended the wedding, until the procession forms once again to walk to the home of the groom.

Once there, the groom's mother stands on the threshold and places the wedding cake for a moment on the head of her son, to compound the luck already gained by borrowed tie and shawl and donation of shillings. The newlyweds dance together alone before the first dance figure is formed, but they spend most of the night seated side by side, talking to well wishers, while music, song, and dance joyously abound in the adjoining kitchen. Presents are given the couple only by kin who have emigrated and by outsiders who have known the two long and well; the same tradition holds true at Christmas among older children and adults. The wedding party, as the *cleamhnas*, may go on night after night, and so may the third party making up the marriage cycle a month later—the "dragging home," which is celebrated at the bride's former house. The term dragging home is employed when either the vernacular or English are spoken, but the word wedding, and its Irish equivalent *bainis*, are used interchangeably in both tongues. Although the bride must not enter her parents' house for a month after the nuptials, she is free to visit with them elsewhere.

The Family and Kinship

There are 79 inhabitable houses in Inis Beag, although many others of hoary vintage still stand and have been converted into outbuildings. Only 71 of these are lived in by the folk, however; 6 of the other 8 (1 of which houses the Dane) recently have been deserted by emigrants, and the remaining 2 are lived in by the curate and the headmaster. The following is a chart showing the categories of personnel occupying the 71 domiciles:

Number of Households	Personnel
30	Husband, wife, and offspring
5	Husband, wife, offspring, and the husband's widowed mother
4	Husband and wife who are childless
4	Husband, wife, offspring, and both parents of the husband
3	Husband, wife, offspring, and the husband's unmarried sister
2	Husband and wife who are childless and both parents of the husband
1	Husband, wife, offspring, and the husband's father who is a widower
1	Husband, wife, offspring, and both parents of the husband and his unmarried sister
1	Husband and wife whose offspring have emigrated
7	Widow and her unmarried offspring
5	Single man (bachelor)
2	Brother and sister both of whom are unmarried
2	Two brothers and a sister all of whom are unmarried
2	Widower and his unmarried offspring
1	Two bachelor brothers
1	Bachelor and his widowed sister-in-law

Implicit in these statistics are such Irish phenomena as monogamy, the predominance of the nuclear family (Only 10.3 percent are extended in Inis Beag.), family exogamy, patrilocal residence, and a high incidence of celibacy. The last listed bachelor who lives with his widowed sister-in-law, and frequently is visited by a brother's adolescent grandson from the mainland, is regarded by many bachelors as fortunate—"He has a woman and a boy to work and no 'responsibilities.'"

Inheritance in the island is patrilineal, and before a man can marry, his father or widowed mother must "pass on" the property to him. To encourage aged men to surrender ownership of their land, a statute forbids their receiving the old age at 70 years until they have so acted. But despite this law, six Inis Beag elders aged 70 to 79 years—with a total of seven bachelor sons ranging in age from 32 to 47 years (not counting eight others who have emigrated but are eligible to inherit) —still maintain ownership themselves. When a man is without sons, he most commonly wills the land to a brother's son or arranges to have a man wed his daughter and "marry in" to the household. An in-marrying son-in-law, it is interesting to note, may pay a bride wealth, which usually is much larger than the dowry of the girl, for he has no land of his own. Among contemporary landholders, five have obtained property from uncles, six from widowed mothers, and two by marrying in. Other land in Inis Beag has been procured through purchase, exchange, gift–giving, and land dispute verdicts.

A major cause of celibacy, late marriage, disputes, and emigration related to the system of inheritance, seldom mentioned either in writings about Inis Beag or by the islanders, is the common practice of a father playing off his sons against one another for the patrimony in order to achieve favored treatment for his wife and himself in their waning years. Elders are well treated, in part as a result of the above and in part out of the fear that after death their ghosts will punish those who have maltreated them. Often the playing off of sons for the patrimony leads to factionalism within the family and may provoke a secretly favored son to emigrate or, more seriously, all sons acting in concert to depart in anger and disgust. Today, a total of 22 married men, widowers, and widows whose average age is 65.7, hold land that is inheritable by a total of 56 sons whose average age is 30.1 years. (The 16 elders who have a total of 20 sons in the island average 66.7 years of age and their offspring 33.6.) The uncertainty about which sibling will inherit is reflected in these figures: of the 59 present landholders, 47 percent are first born, 42 percent second, 8 percent third, and 3 percent fourth and beyond.

Although the Inis Beag family is totally exogamous, the village is only 78.3 percent exogamous (The range for the four villages is from 75 to 83 percent.). Since 1911, six women have married men, mostly farmers, living in communities along the neighboring coast and only one an Inis Thiar islander, while four mainland and five Inis Thiar women have wed men from Inis Beag. During this same 50 year period, six local men have married into contiguous mainland settlements and one into Inis Thiar, but no men from the outside have married into the island. As we have noted already, immigrants for two or three generations are regarded as strangers by the folk, and the same is true of in-marrying wives; these women are treated aloofly and are the victims of much spiteful gossip. Many female siblings marry locally rather than emigrate—one case of four sisters, five of three sisters, and ten of two—and they tend to visit together often and lend mutual economic and emotional support.

When a man marries, his parents relinquish the holding, and its direction passes into the hands of the newlyweds. Arensberg and Kimball talk of the "west room" complex, which may exist in many parts of peasant Ireland but does not in Inis Beag. Houses in north and west Co. Clare "with remarkable uniformity" are aligned east and west, and on the son's marriage the old couple moves into the westernmost room "behind the hearth." This room is linked with the Celtic supernatural, for fairy paths are thought to be located along the western side of many houses, and the pagan afterworld—the Isle of the Blest—is a sunken land mass in the nearby western sea (Arensberg and Kimball 1940:134–136). In Inis Beag, on the contrary, over one-third of the domiciles since 1841 have been aligned north and south, fairy trails are found mostly at the back of the island, and a retiring couple may choose any of three rooms (or more in modern homes) to move into. The west room of Co. Clare is called simply "the room" in Inis Beag.

Thirty-four of the 71 inhabited buildings in the island have thatched roofs (see Fig. 8), while the others are antiquated houses which lately have been renovated, mainly by replacing thatch with slate, or are newly built. The last of the traditional "cabins" or "cottages" were constructed in the 1930s, and the first of the modern ones during the 1890s—with two stories initially, and styled and subsidized by the Congested Districts Board. Old and renovated houses are rectangular in shape, are constructed of whitewashed stones with concrete floors, and have a large central kitchen with doors or half-doors to the outside both front and back. "The room" is beyond the kitchen at one end of the building, and two bedrooms (one in the most ancient cabins) are at the other. Lofts for sleeping are in the gable of the roof above "the room" and bedrooms, and are entered by ladder or staircase from the kitchen. Fireplaces share a common wall and chimney between the kitchen and "the room," as they also may between the two bedrooms; but the kitchen hearth is the most used, and in some homes is not permitted to die out.

The space between the cottage and the low stone wall and outbuildings surrounding it is called the "street." Outbuildings at the back include a toilet and various storage sheds—for spuds and turf sods in particular, although the latter often are stacked instead against a gable of the cabin. In a portion of the street or a small field beyond the wall, a garden for vegetables is maintained for easy access. The kitchen doors of the house sometimes open into small halls in the front or back, or both, and when the weather is not too cold or blustery, the door opening to the street on the windward side is kept closed and its opposite open. In the kitchen, which is the center of family activities, are: the fireplace at which cooking is done with pot and cooking ovens hung from an iron hook; the table around which the family eats their five daily meals; the sideboard, known as a "dresser," filled with "delph"—both everyday and "best" china; the religious shrine with "blessed lamp" surrounded by religious pictures and sacred objects; and, occasionally, a "settlebed" which, when closed, serves as a bench during the daytime.

The hearth in the kitchen is indented into the wall to provide two hobs, or seats, and on a chilly or dampish day the folk will nestle inside the fireplace and sit tightly together on a bench drawn up close to the turf fire for warmth. This fireplace has a profound psychological significance in Inis Beag and, in a sense, is a force drawing the family together. Now that only three hookers transport peat from the mainland—when in the past there had been more than a hundred—and the price of turf increases considerably year by year, coal or bottled gas stoves are being used by most families. Although coal and gas are cheaper to burn, and coal throws out more heat than turf, the coal fire in the hearth does not foster camaraderie as does the peat fire. The replacement of fireplace by stove and the "stink" and dirtiness of coal are denounced incessantly by the islanders, and the disappearance of the "sweet smell" of burning sods and a multitude of customs associated for generations with the peat fire are lamented.

Many functions are served by "the room." It can accommodate the dis-placed parents after their son has married, if all agree, for it has a bed which can serve them (as well as distinguished guests, spectators at parties, and now tourists and summer language school students). This chamber is the best kept of the house, with the newest and most valuable of the furniture and often a linoleum floor, and its walls and ceiling are whitewashed or painted frequently. Family heirlooms and objects of sentimental value, which are parted with only as a last resort, are found here. Religious pictures adorn the walls, and on the mantel over the fire-place are photographs of the family going back generations, especially of those who have emigrated or are deceased. When "the stations" are performed every two decades in the cottage, the mass is read in "the room," and certain rubrics used in this ritual are afterward kept here. Finally, the chamber serves as a dance floor when the crowd at a party in the house overflows the bounds of kitchen, hall, and street.

The social universe of the islanders is divided into four segments: close kin or "friends" (Previously, I have used this word in the American sense.), dis-tant kin or "those I have a relationship with," other islanders, and outsiders or strangers. "Friends" normally extend generationally to include ego's parents, grand-parents, children, and grandchildren, and collaterally to include his affines (spouse's kinsmen), siblings, and first, second, and third cousins—termed, respectively, "four-of-kin," "six-of-kin," and "eight-of-kin."[1] With the intensification of inbreeding, most of the folk are eight-of-kin, and this is why the parish priest examines the genealogies of families at the time of the match. Marriage between first cousins is forbidden, between second cousins demands permission from the bishop, and between third the consent of the parish priest. Distant kin are relatives extended collaterally beyond eight-of-kin, while outsiders include the curates, teachers who are not islanders, lighthouse keepers, the Dane, tourists of local renown, and, as I have just indicated, even in-marrying women and descendants of recently arrived immigrants (also, of course, inquisitive anthropologists).

Although inheritance and succession are patrilineal on the island, descent is bilateral—traced through both agnatic (father's) and uterine (mother's) lines

---

[1] These positions are pictured horizontally (generationally) and vertically (collaterally) in block form in Arensberg and Kimball 1940:96 in the chapter "Kinship System." The Irish kinship system is common to peoples of Western Europe and America (the Eskimo type), and much of the kinship information reported by Arensberg and Kimball applies to Inis Beag.

—with a strong agnatic bias. Rights and duties are distributed among cognates, but they are less strong among uterine and affinal kin, as well as among relatives of both lines according to distance from ego. Rights and duties include obligations to assist and defend, and mutual assistance in Inis Beag characterizes farming, fishing, housebuilding, unloading turf, carrying the coffin at a funeral, and many other activities. Reciprocation in some form for services rendered is almost an obsession among both kin and non-kin, and not to reciprocate adequately means to lose face. The matter of mutual defense will be considered in later sections and chapters.

Only 13 surnames are represented on the island, and there are 27 families bearing a single one, 11 bearing another, and 8 a third. Most Christian names are those of the Blessed Virgin and of saints, especially from the Irish past. Michael, Patrick, Sean (which often is transformed into John, although Eoin is John in Irish), Thomas, Martin, Peter, Coleman, and Joseph—in that order—are the most popular first names for males, while for females it is Mary, Brigid, Margaret, Ann, Catherine, Sarah, Nora, and Teresa. In the past, it was customary for Inis Beag women to bear their offspring at home attended by nurse, midwife, or skilled female relative; but during the past decade, most infants have been delivered in the mainland hospital serving the island, where mothers have learned of "different" surnames and have assigned them to their own children—such as Gerard, Xavier, Christopher, and Pius for boys, and Rita, Carmel, Veronica, and Jude for girls.

Each person in the island has a term of reference which never is employed as a term of address.[2] For a man, it is a nickname or his Christian name followed by that of his father: "The General" or Sean Michael. Women ordinarily are not given nicknames; if single, they append their father's first name to their own, and if married, their husband's. An adult man may bear the Christian name of his mother following his own rather than his father's, if, for instance, his mother was widowed early or unduly dominated her husband. Nicknames relate to such things as occupations, abodes, personality idiosyncracies, stature, color of hair, and events of the past; and many are uncomplimentary to the degree of fomenting disputes if uttered at improper times or to inappropriate persons.

Before turning to reciprocal relationships which exist between certain agnatic, uterine, and affinal relatives, it is necessary to examine two phenomena which have a vital bearing on kinship and other behavior: the Oedipus complex and male solidarity. Fr. Alexander J. Humphreys says that there is in Ireland a ". . . centripetal mechanism built into the fabric of rural life. This is the strong, preferential love of the rural mother for her sons. She is a magnetic center of the family and her cohesive power is affection. This love, which leads her 'to slave' for her sons and to demand that her daughters do likewise, cushions the sons' hard lot. It mollifies the constant rub of his subordination to his father . . ."

---

[2] A term of reference is a name used to refer to a person who is not present, while a term of address is a name used to address a person to his face. In America, one might say in referring to his mother, "That woman walking toward us is my mother.", and then greet her as she joins the group, "Hi, Mom."; in this case, mother is a term of reference and Mom a term of address. Often terms of address in the Western world are Christian names, and some terms of reference and address may be identical. Anthropologists usually collect only terms which are used to designate various kin.

(Humphreys 1965:245). A far more forceful statement is that of Marvin K. Opler and Jerome L. Singer, wherein they address the etiology and consequences of the Oedipus configuration in the Irish family:

> The central figure in Irish families is more likely to be a controlling figure on the distaff side, while fathers, especially in straitened economic circumstances, are frequently by contrast shadowy and evanescent.... An Irish male ... beset with anxiety and fear of female figures early in life, and lacking possibilities of firm male identification with a father, would later experience the sexual repressions and socio-religious definitions of marriage and sexuality for which his culture, with its high celibacy rates, protracted engagements, and sin-guilt emphasis, is justly famous.... all this spells a final anxious and fearful lack of positive sexual identification, varying in a continuum from repressed and latent homosexual balances through to added displacements and distortions that are either pallid asexuality or fearful and bizarre misidentifications.... Irish resistance to role identification ... was seen as ... having the imprint of anxiety in relations with persons of the opposite sex, ordinarily mothers and older sisters.... [The] ... basic personality has stamped into it such feelings as male inadequacy, the masculine protest, hostility toward females, and the kind of latent homosexual feelings which produce a further sense of sin and guilt ... (Opler and Singer 1956:15–18).

Complementing the Oedipus complex is male solidarity, which has a long history in Ireland—revealed in legend, historical sources, and modern literature. Psychologists of Freudian bent see male solidarity as one of the many behavioral manifestations of the Oedipus configuration—based on "male inadequacy, the masculine protest, hostility toward females," and "latent homosexual feelings;" but many anthropologists (especially functionalists) analyze it as a sociocultural phenomenon, for it is found in societies where the Oedipus complex appears not to exist. Elizabeth Coxhead, in discussing Lady Gregory's play, *Grania* (completed in 1912), alludes to the "tragic plight" of many Irish women, past and present:

> *Grania* is ... a play in which a woman is ousted from an emotional relationship between two men. The "love" is that of man for man, of brother for brother; it is loyalty to the warrior band, and a corresponding resentment of the woman who takes away the warrior's freedom, makes trouble with his comrades, distracts him from his purpose in life. It is an attitude which filters through the play as light filters through crystal; which runs through the heroic Irish sagas ... Its continuing validity was borne out by all Lady Gregory had observed in the world around her, the world of the "loveless Irishman," the peasant society which relegated women to serfdom, the middle-class intellectual society which left them only donkey-work.... it is not Finn alone who robs Grania of Diarmuid. "His desire was all the time with you yourself, and Almhuin." Almhuin, the charmed circle of hunters and warriors; its modern equivalent was the masculine society of clubs and bars, of wit and talk and stimulus, from which a woman ... would be forever excluded ... such a view of the Irishwoman's role, of her relegation to insignificance and her resentment under it, is not exclusively feminine. It is abundantly confirmed by Synge. His heroines ... are creatures caged and raging, given no scope for their powers, condemned to love men who are poor things beside them and do not really care for them at all.... A woman has only to put her nose into a saloon bar ... to realize that Almhuin is with us still (Coxhead 1961:145–146).

Marriage figures prominently as a provision of economic welfare in folk societies throughout the world, and this is illustrated in Inis Beag by two statements made to me by middle-aged, married men: one said that marriage is a matter of "making a good living," and the other that the attributes of an ideal wife are, "She keeps the fire going, has the tea ready, and listens to a man's troubles." Performing economic tasks, satisfying sexual needs, and rearing children are the *raison d'etre* for women according to most island men, but this does not mean that affection between spouses is lacking. The relationship between most mates, however, is one of "accommodation," and the affection, if present, lacks depth. It is said that "husbands and wives never walk together;" but my wife and I have observed two couples who often fail to observe this dictum, between whom conjugal love as defined in the Western tradition appears to exist. Intimate communication between mates is rare, as it is between most folk—including even mothers and sons and those who are allied through institutionalized friendship. Several disputing husbands and wives have not spoken to one another, except formally, for many years. In the case of disputes of this sort—as well as those involving other kin in the household—the parties involved limit as much as possible both contact and cooperation between themselves rather than resort to abusive argument. Physical assault is unusual, but that the repressed wish to perpetrate violence may be widespread is attested by the delirious response of the islanders to the plot of John M. Synge's play, *The Playboy of the Western World*, when related to them; in it peasants of Co. Mayo laud the youthful "playboy, Christy" for apparently "slaying his da" (father) with a "loy" (spade). The act which so horrified viewers of nativistic persuasion in Dublin and Boston half a century ago arouses the opposite effect among the folk.

Women commonly express jealousy of and resentment against not only what they consider the less time consuming and stressful work load of men, but also the greater freedom enjoyed by their husbands. Many times women confided to my wife that they are greatly distressed at being forced to remain home minding their children and performing tedious household chores, while their spouses range the entire island and the sea about it in their economic pursuits and are involved in numerous social activities forbidden by custom to women. Some of these same women expressed deep concern over being compelled by the unauthorized decree of local curates, as well as by the sexual demands of their mates, to produce as many offspring as possible; they complained that the constant bearing and rearing of children increase their work, restrict their freedom, and perpetuate the poverty of their families. Few men whom we questioned were aware—or were willing to admit—that such sentiments are held by their wives, but most men cited as one of the more attractive aspects of local life their being bossed by no one and being able to shift from one job to another among a wide variety to avoid boredom. Men are away from their homes much of the time, day and night, and they do far more "social" walking about the island, visiting relatives and acquaintances, and going to Inis Thiar and the mainland than do their spouses. Also, they frequent the pubs and attend the summer *céilí* on the common land, which married women do not.

Despite sexual repression and the complaints of wives about large families, children are much desired by parents, and the fertility rate in Inis Beag is extremely high. An examination of 109 marriages between 1891 and 1960 reveals that the average number of offspring per couple is 6.4 (7.2 for marriages in which the wife has passed the menopause); this figure excludes spouses who are barren. The range in family size is between 1 and 16 offspring, and 18 of the 109 marriages have produced 7 children—the modal unit. Today, 6 couples are childless and as a result are "pitied" by their neighbors, who hold that it is the females who are sterile. At least 2 women, to my wife's knowledge, have been examined by obstetricians on the mainland and been found fecund; but they have been unable to persuade their spouses of the medical fact or get them to consult the doctors themselves. Men are anxious about their own maleness, as evidenced in the ability to produce offspring in this case, and have an eye to aid in their labors and to descent, succession, and inheritance. Women desire children, in part, to compensate for the lack of attention and affection from their mates.

Most of the enculturation during infancy and childhood in Inis Beag is done by mothers, as men are away much of the time and, if at home, "don't like to mind the kids." Mothers favor their sons, whom they "overprotect" and to whom they give "seductive" care. In the process of childrearing, sexual interest is first elicited and then blocked by punishing its behavioral manifestations. As a result of the mother's close ties to the male child, the father often is alienated from familial interaction, is hostile toward the youth, and fails to become a source of firm masculine attachment. Disliking to fulfill the responsibilities of enculturation and often in conflict with both his wife and male offspring, the father forces his mate to project herself into her role as childrearer to gain solace, and thus the cycle repeats itself. Although fathers tend to favor their daughters, their desire to "escape" the home discourages a pronounced Electra complex from arising. The bond between mother and son is so binding that it is not infrequent for marriage to be postponed after the death of the father, and the son to work the holding for his widowed mother until he has reached the age of confirmed bachelorhood. "This is also the basis for the conflict between mother-in-law and daughter-in-law that is quite intense in Ireland, the prospect of which leads so many sons to refuse 'to bring another woman in on my mother'" (Humphreys 1965:246).

Within marriage, husbands tend to relate themselves to their wives as they have to their mothers when single. The wife is the "strong" person in the household, on whom the husband is emotionally dependent even when their relationship is one of mutual withdrawal and uncooperativeness. In most households, the wife shares at least equally in decision-making, and in many the husband bows to his spouse's decisions, not only in minor matters but in affairs of utmost importance to the family and those relating to activities normally within the male sphere, such as farming. It is the wife who invariably handles the money in the household. Freudians would see the influence of the mother image in the realm of sex: the rarity of conjugal love, the lack of sexual foreplay marked by little or no concern with the female breast, the brevity of the coital act and the frequent spurning of the woman following it, the need to degrade the female in the sexual act, and the belief that the "good" women does not enjoy sex and, conversely, that the sexually responsive woman is by virtue of the fact "evil."[3]

As might be expected, there is much sibling rivalry in the island. Between brothers, the major factors responsible are competition for the affection of the mother and for the patrimony; the latter condition adds fuel to the fire of disputes between many sons and their fathers. Competition for the mother's affection is also an important cause of rivalry between brothers and sisters, particularly when the love of the mother for her sons leads her "to slave" for them and "to demand that her daughters do likewise." But the early separation of the sexes and inculcation of male solidarity contribute as well to this antagonism. In some families, affectional ties between children and their grandparents—both agnatic and uterine—are closer than other kinship bonds, with the exception of that between mothers and sons. The grandmother in the extended family plays a considerable role in childrearing, even when the relationship between herself and her daughter-in-law is strained, which is usual; and children often visit the home of their mother's parents, where they are treated indulgently.

The displaced parents in the joint family draw into the background reluctantly and with considerable difficulty. Writing of the folk of Co. Clare, Arensberg and Kimball say:

> Where the transition goes smoothly, father and son continue to work the farm together, but more often as the father grows older he retires to his seat by the hearth. . . . The coming-in of the daughter-in-law is sometimes not so harmonious. Disputes arise. . . In such cases, the mediations of the parish priest and public opinion generally patch up a compromise, but, as far as the authors have observed, the transition is a gradual and successful one. The young woman usually serves a sort of apprenticeship at the hands of the mother-in-law . . . and at least during the young woman's childbearing years the older one maintains her control (Arensberg and Kimball 1940:123–124).

The transition is far less smooth in the island; fathers work less with their sons and retire sooner to the hearth (and the bed); and the apprenticeship of the in-marrying woman seldom extends beyond the birth of her first child. Disputes between grandparents and parents in the extended family of Inis Beag appear to be more numerous than in Co. Clare.

Disputes

Disputes between kin and non-kin in Irish communities have been studied seldom until very recently. In reading what writers and social scientists have written about peasant Ireland in general, and Inis Beag in particular, one often is led to the conclusion that disputes are rare or altogether lacking. Nativism and primitivism have caused many observers to present this distorted picture of social

---

[3] I must stress the provisional nature of these data on sex, and those to follow on p. 110, for they are based on a limited sample of men and women respondents and relate to the cultural area of most circumspection.

harmony, but other biases are at work (Messenger 1968:29–30). Writers of strong religious bent have exaggerated the Catholic moral virtues embodied in the Irish family and community and have disregarded disputes because they involve unchristian behavior, while social scientists with a functional theoretical orientation have emphasized the integration of social groups and have neglected disputes because they betray dysfunction. Those observers who have depended almost entirely on the guided interview to obtain data concerning family and community often have remained oblivious to disputes. Some researchers, however, have collected information on disputes in an objective manner, but have been unwilling to publish it for fear of antagonizing the folk, the church, and the government—thus losing their positions or jeopardizing research in the future. The most valuable study to date on disputes in Ireland is that of Elliott Leyton, which is based on research that he conducted between 1964 and 1966 in Aughnaboy (like Inis Beag, a fictitious name), a village in Co. Down with three times the population of Inis Beag.

Using Claude Lévi-Strauss' distinction between conscious and unconscious models, Leyton first examines the conscious models—explanatory constructs, or norms, of the people themselves—held by Aughnaboy villagers concerning disputes, then the types of disputes which in fact do occur within the community —from which the unconscious models are inferred by the analyst. Three conscious models held by the villagers are of pertinence to us: those for personal conduct, relations between kinsmen, and relations between non-kin (Leyton 1966:535– 536). The first is summarized in the concept of "decency."

> To be a "decent" man is to carry out one's obligations to society in a style characterized by cheerfulness and friendliness, to pause willingly for a chat and, most importantly, to refrain—regardless of the provocation—from any display of overt hostility. . . . greatest esteem is reserved for those who succeed in maintaining cordial relations with everyone in the village; and the greatest contempt is reserved for those quarrelsome individuals who are frequently involved in disputes.

Relations between kinsmen, Leyton says,

> . . . are characterized, ideally, by the highest degree of friendliness and harmony. The individual is expected to feel the strongest affection for his kinsmen, and to subordinate all other loyalties . . . to the demands of his kinsmen. . . . individuals are expected to suppress their personal desires and ideals if they conflict with the unity of the group. . . . Close affective ties and regular visiting rarely occur outside the field of kinship. Non-kin are regarded with suspicion and distrust, and the interests of non-kin are seen as being in potential opposition to the interests of one's own kin.

Ideally, friendliness and harmony characterize relations between non-kin as well in Aughnaboy.

> Non-kin are in general expected to behave according to the standards of "decency" . . . to be cheerful and talkative and to avoid quarrels. . . . Aughnaboy inhabitants conceive relations between non-kin to be a system in equilibrium . . . relations

between the separate groups of kin in the village are seen to be in delicate balance of power which is expressed in the local phrase, "you can't fight anybody around here because all their people will gang up on you." If an individual's kinsmen must defend him in his personal disputes, it necessarily follows that a clash between two individuals soon becomes a clash between two groups of kin.

By and large, these three conscious models apply to Inis Beag as well as Aughnaboy. Leyton discovers broad "disparities between the conscious models and the statistical patterns formed by the actual behaviour" of people in Aughnaboy, manifested in 74 disputes covering a time span of ten years in the memories of his respondents. He classifies these disputes according to three criteria: their severity, the issues provoking them, and the categories of individuals involved (Leyton 1966:537–539). The criterion of severity yields three types of disputes: argument —"characterized by frequent or continuous arguments . . . associated primarily with exchange of verbal abuse;" withdrawal—where "social relations are actually severed and cooperation is withdrawn;" and interference—in which active attempts are made to "interfere with the welfare of the opposing party. These attempts, which may be secret or open, include legal suits, reports to the police, theft and, rarely, physical violence, as well as withdrawal of all cooperation." Three types of disputes also are distinguishable when issues provoking hostility are examined: economic—"which includes conflict such as rivalry between shopkeepers and disputed inheritance;" personality clashes—"which includes disputes primarily attributed to the innately quarrelsome personalities of certain individuals;" and jealousy—"which refers primarily to situations in which an individual's affections are alienated." The categories of persons involved in disputes are agnatic kin, uterine kin, affinal kin, and non-kin. Leyton establishes rank orders for each of his type classifications, and finds that the rank order for the severity classification is withdrawal, interference, and argument; for the issues classification, it is personality clashes, jealousy, and economic; and for the individuals involved classification, it is affinal kin, agnatic kin, non-kin, and uterine kin.

In applying Leyton's unconscious models of disputes to Inis Beag, I have modified slightly his severity and issues classifications. To the former, I have added a fourth type which I call gossip; this is not gossip of the ordinary variety so common on the island, but rather continuous, pernicious verbal attacks made by a person within earshot of his victim's relatives and close friends, which usually do not lead to argument. In the case of the issues classification, I have broadened the range of personality clashes. There are several "innately quarrelsome" individuals in Inis Beag, but most personality conflicts involve persons other than these, who have come to dislike one another intensely for numerous reasons, most of which are related to envy, jealousy (other than alienation of affections), resentment against authority, and hostility toward members of the opposite sex. Over 200 disputes have occurred on the island within the past generation, excluding those involving semi-permanent dwellers—curates, lighthouse keepers, and the Dane. The higher incidence of disputes in Inis Beag is attributable, for the most part, to the longer time span appraised and the addition of gossip to the severity classification in my analysis. However, the rank orders of the three type classifications closely approximate those for Aughnaboy; only the severity classification in Inis Beag differs, with gossip most prevalent followed by withdrawal, argument, and interference.

A further step in Leyton's analysis is his examination of the severity of disputes and the issues provoking them with relation to the four categories of persons involved. Jealousy and personality clashes, in that order, are the causes of disputes between affinal kin in Aughnaboy, which give rise to withdrawal and argument. In the case of agnatic kin, the causes are personality clashes and economic conflict, and withdrawal and argument are the sole responses; the same causes apply to disputes between non-kin, but interference rather than withdrawal is by far the most conspicuous response. Disputes between uterine kin are negligible. These rank orders are in accord with those of Inis Beag except for the predominance of interference in disputes between non-kin; on the island, gossip and withdrawal outweigh interference. The major disputes in Inis Beag are: between spouses and between mothers and daughters-in-law among affinal kin; between fathers and sons, between brothers, and between brothers and sisters among agnatic kin; and between families, between shopkeepers, and between particular individuals who are distantly or not related. Since disputes between agnatic, uterine, and affinal kin have been discussed in the last two sections, I will consider here only disputes between non-kin.

At least eight family disputes are ongoing in Inis Beag today, one of which has roots in events of a century ago (Another is supported by the exhortations of a ghost, as we shall see in the next chapter.). All are the result of past and present contests over the ownership and inheritance of land, and of past personality clashes which have led to violent argument and interference, especially physical violence, and have come to involve near cognates of the original enemies—"a clash between two individuals soon becomes a clash between two groups of kin." This type of factionalism gives rise mostly to gossip and the avoidance of one another by members of the contending families; only on rare occasions, usually at large social gatherings after much drink has been taken by the men, will disputants engage in face-to-face argument, which soon can provoke fighting between two and sometimes more persons. Fights are short-lived, inasmuch as other islanders, the headmaster, or the priest intervene to redress "the delicate balance of power . . . between the separate groups of kin." Legal suits over land ownership and inheritance have been many during the past three decades, and on several occasions guards have been summoned to Inis Beag by feuding families to investigate cases of physical violence and the destruction of property. Theft as a form of interference is practically unknown on the island. Economic conflict and the clash of personalities also underlie the dispute between the two shopkeepers, and gossip and withdrawal characterize their relationship, just as that between members of disputing families.

Since most of the folk in Inis Beag are related at least distantly, the term non-kin denotes both "those I have a relationship with" and those who are unrelated. Leyton finds that most non-kin disputes in Aughnaboy involve at least one person who has no effective kin; this situation does not exist in the island where everyone has effective kin. By far the greatest number of disputes between non-kin in Inis Beag occur between members of the same sex and involve men rather than women. They arise largely out of personality clashes and are expressed in gossip and withdrawal. As in Aughnaboy, none of the disputes between men appear to be based on competition for women, although jealousy of a rival and anger at being rejected have spurred a few disputes involving particular women and couples. One of the important causes of personality conflict in the island is the dogmatism of the folk. They are quick to form opinions, often on the basis of inadequate information, and cling tenaciously to them once they are voiced publicly. Thus, a simple difference of views concerning a topic between two persons can grow into a serious altercation lasting a lifetime—and beyond. One facet of this dogmatism is the local belief that the character of a person can be assessed accurately on first meeting him. I became the victim of a dispute of sorts by telling a man that my "first impressions" of a new acquaintance often are wrong, and that I prefer to interact for some time with the individual before passing judgment on him; this admittance branded me as deficient in character and one to be "withdrawn" from, and I never made it again.

I have mentioned that dependence on the guided interview can prevent an observer from gaining insight into disputes among Irish and Inis Beag peasants; this is so because dysfunctional social relations are kept carefully hidden from outsiders—the conscious models concerning disputes not only are incorporated into the self-image of the islanders but are urged on strangers. The concern for kin, acquaintances, and particular groups manifested in speech and behavior, which at times can be most sentimental, cannot be taken at face value. The emigrating relative whose departure provokes tears on the strand may be forgotten quickly, and his absence even heralded, in the privacy of the home, and the mourners at a graveside may include many who display indifference when thought to be unobserved while kneeling in the rear ranks. This state of affairs gives rise to a brief consideration of the problems associated with procuring reliable data.

Honor Tracy, in the first chapter (aptly entitled "Forebodings") of her book, *Mind You I've Said Nothing*, humorously predicts the various reactions that her volume will stimulate in Irish readers She concludes with the following statement about the difficulties surrounding fact-finding in Ireland:

> This question of fact was another of the spectres hovering in my path. In every book there should be a fact here and there or the writer is charged with aimless frivolity. But facts in Ireland are very peculiar things. They are rarely allowed to spoil the sweep and flow of conversation: the crabbing effect they have on good talk is eliminated almost entirely. I do not believe myself that the Irishman conveniently ignores their existence, as sometimes is said, so much as that he is blithely unaware of it. He soars above their uninviting surfaces on the wing of his fancy. Who then would answer my questions truthfully, who would supply me with that modicum of sober and accurate information required to give my book a serious air? No one, as far as I knew. And if facts are elusive and shadowy things in Ireland, opinions are more so. An Irishman ... will say not what he thinks but what he believes you would like him to think; he is a man of honeyed words, anxious to flatter and soothe, cajole and caress ... [He does not] reveal his own true thoughts if, to be sure, he has any. He would be in dread lest you quoted him and the story went around and he got the name of a bold outspoken fellow, which might be bad for business. And then again so many Irishmen find an innocent glee in misleading and deceiving for its own sake.

> Obfuscation is the rule, and while it may seem a little foolish at times, there is no
> doubt that it makes for a great deal of fun. It cultivates too a sharpness of ear, a
> feeling for half-tones and shades and subtleties, and a wary alertness that would
> be worth its weight in gold should one ever be lost in a jungle (Tracy 1953:20–
> 21).

The quotation in some measure applies to interviewing in Inis Beag, where my wife
and I took great pains to disentangle real from ideal culture by substantiating interview data with observation wherever possible.

The existence of the conditions depicted by Tracy, as well as the numerous
cultural practices shrouded in secrecy, led us to return to the island several times
after 1960 before I attempted this book, to emphasize various modes of participant observation, to devise *ad hoc* research methods of an unorthodox nature,
to "hone" our orthodox tools and employ cross-checking techniques at every stage
of our project, and to cultivate that "sharpness of ear . . . feeling for half-tones
and shades and subtleties, and . . . wary alertness" which so distinguishes ethnographic endeavor as an art as well as a systematic epistemology. The use by many
folk of "wings of fancy," "honeyed words," and "obfuscations"—popularly known
as "blarney"—reflects a long tradition of verbal skill. It is a vital component of
Irish and Inis Beag "charm," which often is the product of a delicately poised set
of defense mechanisms; beneath it can lie feelings of inferiority and dislike, envy,
and jealousy of others. Blarney can serve very effectively to shield genuine thoughts
and feelings and thus defend the ego. Irish folklore and literature also reflect this
tradition, and it is probably expressed most formidably in James Joyce's *Ulysses*
and *Finnegan's Wake* (At least one Irish folklorist has collected "Joycean" utterances from peasants.).

Prestige Status

Inis Beag lacks a class system, and the status symbols which affect human
relationships are few. That land and capital—known collectively as "money,"
"wealth," or "riches"—are the major symbols is revealed in the frequently heard
phrase, "If you have money and your health, you're all right." (Health alone is
mentioned by those of lesser means.). The men of highest prestige are the king
and the 13 who own 24 or more acres of land. But they and their families do not
interact more with one another than with others, for, as we have noted, the web
of kinship rather than the possession of status attributes largely determines who
will interact with whom and in what manner. Nor is their style of life different
from that of other islanders, since material possessions and social etiquette are
relatively unimportant in the status system. Although the king is a "man of few
gardens," his capital, charismatic personality, and "connections" with priests,
politicians, and civil servants earn him his high position in the status hierarchy.
The prestige which comes with land ownership is based more on the fact of its
possession than on the potential wealth that it represents. Men with large holdings
can, of course, build more fields and on the increased acreage raise more cattle and
sheep and grow more surplus crops for sale, but few take advantage of this oppor-

tunity to create additional capital; they are content to rest on their psychological laurels, are limited in their aspirations, and are indolent. They betray a smugness of attitude much resented by their less prestigeful fellows. A woman spoke contemptuously of the "great estates" boasted of by these men, when she discussed with me the many land disputes that she had witnessed during her lifetime.

When one asks the folk to rank prestige symbols and the positions of individuals in the status hierarchy, the only consensus which emerges is the placing of land and capital at the apex of the rank order of symbols, the assigning of men who possess these in greatest quantity to the top of the hierarchy, and the placing of landless men at the bottom. Least prestigeful among the landless are those who are descendants of fisherfolk, most of whose families were recent migrants to Inis Beag. An example of the verbal abuse to which they are subjected is a remark made to one of them by the king in a heated argument, who said, "Why don't you spend your time gathering periwinkles like your father?"; the man replied with equal venom, "Who was your father, a king?" Other prestige symbols delineated by the folk, although not mentioned by all and variously ranked, are advanced education, prestigeful kin abroad, economic skills, and singing, dancing, and storytelling abilities. Strength and courage occasionally are cited, but they are considered symbols of a past era (which nativism and primitivism make difficult to assess) and have come to lose much of their significance.

Only one family in the island prides itself on its material possessions, because of the influence of the householder's brother in the United States who sends remittances, so it is said, and often visits Inis Beag for lengthy stays. I was asked to take photographs of this family, whose members posed before various pieces of modern furniture and appliances, to be sent to relatives—the only such request ever made of me. There are a few families, however, which pride themselves on the neatness and cleanliness of their houses and streets and the appearance of their members, and they are apt to denigrate families which are slovenly. The lack of emphasis on material possessions in Inis Beag presents a startling contrast to the situation which prevails in most of the Western world, including many peasant societies and the mainland Irish; equally contrasting is the apparent lack of opprobrium attached to doing relief work on the roads and receiving the dole.

Although 28 islanders have received some secondary education during the past 15 years (excluding priests and nuns), only 2 have attended university—both of them before the Second World War at University College, Dublin. Two women and a man have become teachers, and the former have returned to Inis Beag to teach in the national school. Most of the advanced students today are preparing to teach or nurse or are gaining technical skills, and it is not expected by their parents that they will return to the island to live permanently. Families are boastful of their members with advanced education, and those families without such representation often urge their children to do better in the local school, and try to muster financial support for their high school education if scholarships are not forthcoming. I was told by a man disgusted with the lack of interest in school shown by his son, "The man who uses a pen is better off than the man who uses a spade or trammel net." Prestige also is gained through having a close relative become a nun or priest or achieve success in the business or professional world, especially outside of Ireland. Four islanders have entered orders—two priests and two nuns—and have brought their families not only prestige but an aura of sanctity; it is believed by the folk that God bestows grace on his earthly representatives and on their kin as well. Even the king is thought to receive some measure of supernatural support for the period of time that he spent during his youth, as is rumored, as a servant at Maynooth Seminary.

The folk rank one another according to their ability to row the *curach*, fish, farm, knit, and perform other economic tasks, although such talents do not bring the prestige that they once did. I often have heard individuals chaffed publicly, sometimes even to their faces, for possessing less than average skills, and many persons have told me privately that they admire or envy the skills of others and wish that they themselves were more adept. A man who owns land in the quarter of another village told me that he works painstakingly in setting a garden there, since his efforts will be appraised by the alien villagers and pitilessly condemned if found wanting. Women gain most of their prestige through performing well the tasks ascribed to them by the division of labor. The economic skills of individuals who lived in the past are lauded more than those of contemporary islanders, reflecting the shift of emphasis in the prestige system; this is far more the case with singing, dancing, and storytelling, as well as with the display of strength and courage. Institutionalized storytelling had disappeared from Inis Beag before 1960, although raconteurs of note still hold forth in the pubs and at small social gatherings. These persons, and the several who excel at singing and dancing, are held in high repute. Probably the best liked of the islanders is a man of 72 years who is admired for his wit, charm, friendliness, and agile step dancing. When drinking in the pubs, he enjoys telling anecdotes about his past experiences, singing and dancing, expressing a simulated sadness at his bachelor estate, and poking sly fun at the behavior of certain folk. Although he is landless and thought to be overly lazy, he is ranked high in the prestige hierarchy because of his esthetic talents and occasional *joie de vivre*. His recluse brother of opposite temperament remarked sadly, "Even the stones of the island know him, but no one knows me." Another landless man, now deceased, who was about the same age, enjoyed high status because he was a traditional storyteller, was noted as a young man for his exceptional strength and athletic and rowing prowess, had spent a decade in the United States, and by reading had educated himself well above the level of most of the folk.

Stories abound concerning once famous men of strength and courageous deeds in Inis Beag and the surrounding region. These anecdotes are recounted more during the summer months than the winter ones, when tourists are within earshot and can be suitably impressed. Acts of courage performed by folk in the past mostly deal with mishaps which occurred to crews while fishing or traveling to and from nearby islands or the mainland. The feats of strength performed by former athletes—such as putting the shot, long jumping, and "throwing the half-hundred"—are well within the realm of possibility, but other feats usually are grossly exaggerated. Examples of the latter are the man who, grasping the base of the front leg of a chair in which sat a person weighing 11 stones (154 pounds), lifted it with one hand, also the man who raised over his head "with ease" a struggling opponent of 16 stones (224 pounds) in a pub fight. A famous writer claimed that he introduced into Inis Beag a feat of agility that he had learned in France, which consists of holding a stick in both hands at the knees and jumping back and forth across it without losing grip; the islanders attest that this "trick" was known locally for at least a century, and one man boasted that his father was able to leap back and forth a dozen times in quick succession. My rapport with the men was enhanced by the fact that I had been a weight thrower and lifter and used to entertain them by putting a granite boulder, throwing a discus that I had brought with me, and performing repetition presses with a barrel of stout. However, the one time that I was persuaded to compete for Inis Beag against Inis Thiar in putting the shot (a flat-bottomed store weight of 14 pounds), I fouled with my foot all three times and thus suffered ignominious defeat. The curate who officiated at the event appeared pleased, but the islanders who had placed wagers on me were of opposite disposition.

4

The Supernatural and the Esthetic

Catholicism

B ECAUSE OF THE WRITINGS OF NATIVISTS, most visitors to Inis Beag believe that the Catholicism of the folk embodies an ideal unattained even on the mainland, where the faith is thought to set an example for all of Christendom. In fact, however, the worship of the islanders is obsessively oriented toward salvation in the next world with a corresponding preoccupation with sin in this world; there is a marked tendency toward polytheism in the manner in which they relate to the Blessed Virgin and certain Irish saints; rituals and sacred artifacts, Christian as well as pagan, often are employed by them to serve magical ends; and, finally, many observances that they hold to be orthodox Catholic are in reality idiosyncratic to Inis Beag or to Ireland. Christian morality in its outward manifestations, as we have seen, is realized to a remarkable degree, but it is less a product of the emphasis placed on good works as a means of gaining salvation than of the techniques of social control exercised by the priests and an overwhelming fear of damnation.

Coexisting with Catholicism in Inis Beag are pre-Celtic, Celtic, and early medieval Christian retentions of religious beliefs and behavior. It is these which are accentuated in the writings of primitivists, some of whom have ignored altogether Catholicism in the lives of the folk. Nativists and primitivists part company in the matter of religion in peasant Ireland, and writers of nativistic persuasion have exerted the most influence on visitors to Inis Beag, who are preponderantly Irish Catholic. Theologians and scholars in Ireland label as pagan unorthodox religious forms from any historical period, and many of these have become reinterpreted with similar Catholic elements. The pagan array of supernatural beings includes a variety of spirits and demons, witches, ghosts, and phantom ships; among other retentions are taboos, signs which foretell the future, charms and incantations of a protective nature, folk medicines, and the aforementioned emphasis on natural foods and other products impinging on the human body.

The islanders know little of church dogma and the purport of rituals and feast days. What knowledge they do possess often is distorted, and they seldom read the Bible or manuals of instruction or engage in doctrinal discussions among themselves. I discovered by consulting priests and church histories, dictionaries, and exegeses—both before and during my stay in Inis Beag—that I came to know far more about the faith than any of the folk, and I sometimes imparted what I had learned to the curious in homes and even in the pubs. Instruction is welcomed by the islanders, but they dislike criticism from any quarter of their idiosyncratic Catholic observances, pagan retentions and reinterpretations, and non–Christian behavior. They also dislike being told, especially by returned emigrants, that "Catholic culture" in Ireland is quite unlike that in other parts of the world and arouses dismay and even incredulity in many foreign Catholics who visit Ireland.

The paths to salvation, according to the islanders, are threefold: obeying the curate, performing the rituals of the church diligently and punctiliously, and conforming to the moral laws of Christianity. Being saved, however, is to them much more a matter of escaping Hell than of achieving Purgatory and eventually Heaven, and they experience more anxiety about failing to conform to the moral laws than pride in conforming to them. Furthermore, it is sins of thought rather than sins of deed which preoccupy them. While they boast of their morality as expressed in behavior, they labor under a heavy burden of guilt arising out of repressed sexual desires, jealousy and envy of their neighbors, and anti-clerical sentiment, among other attitudes. It is difficult for most of them to confess these to the priest, and thus their feelings of guilt and fear of damnation are compounded. Many times in Inis Beag I heard a "good Catholic" defined as one who "thinks mostly of death, Judgment, Heaven, and Hell" and guides his conduct accordingly. Life on earth is regarded as merely a brief prelude to the "eternity stretching beyond the grave," to be lived only in preparation for the Day of Judgment and borne patiently in all its "pain and suffering." Priests and nuns are envied for many reasons, among them the fact that they can "spend most of their time preparing for death" and thus are in a better position to achieve salvation.

It is apparent to outside observers and to the folk alike that women are more pious than men. They attend church more regularly, are more serious of mien at mass and during other religious observances, and are more prone to talk of religious matters than men. Many women go to mass daily, and it is said that all of the women of the island, but only ten men, have evaded going to Hell magically by attending mass nine Fridays in succession after Ash Wednesday (or, according to some, the first Friday in each month for nine successive months, or the first Friday after Ash Wednesday for nine years in succession). The reasons for this are several, but the most important are that women are less contented than men and thus have a greater need for the solace that religion affords, and they are more restricted socially than men and by fulfilling various church obligations can escape household confinement and interact with other women. Some islanders are thought to be overly pious—"wear their religion on their sleeves"—and are subjects of amusement and derision; those who use piety to cloak avarice and other Christian vices are detested and are likely to become the butt of satirical anecdotes and ballads.

In many primitive and peasant societies, in which Christianity has dispossessed polytheistic religions, it has been observed that polytheism has left a legacy whereby the Virgin Mary and various angels and saints are worshipped as dispensers of personal power in their own right. This has been extended to the Trinity among the Anang of Nigeria, who believe that God provided independent power for his human son, Jesus, with which to convert the world to Christianity, and for the Holy Spirit (who has joined the indigenous pantheon of spirits) to act for mankind as healer, prognosticator, forgiver of sins, and protector against ghosts, witches, and sorcerers (Messenger 1959:291). Most Inis Beag folk regard God and the Devil, among Christian supernatural beings, as the only possessors of personal power. But some think that power emanating from the deity is manipulated by the Blessed Virgin and particular saints, and they as well as he must be propitiated for best results. When asked why she prayed to St. Enda rather than to other saints, an old woman said that this saint is "nearer to God" and therefore able to capture more of his power than others. A few islanders hold that these intermediary entities possess power not emanating from the deity, and thus may be approached individually through prayer and sacrifice for their favor. The saints most often appeased are St. Patrick, St. Brigid, St. Enda, and the patron saint of the island.

The Devil is thought to command power for evil as great as or greater than that of the Virgin Mary and the saints for good. Some believe that he controls malevolent pagan beings as well as his own minions from Hell, and he both tempts Christians to sin and attacks them bodily causing sickness, injury, and other misfortunes. He is abroad at all times, although his power is amplified on such occasions as Allhallows' Eve, and sometimes he can be seen by human eyes—as a huge, dark, indistinct figure standing at a distance, usually after nightfall or when it is raining heavily. One evening during a severe storm, I visited without advance notice a man milking his cow at the back of the island, and he would not approach me as I stood atop a fence wearing oilskin and sou'wester until I called out to him and established the fact that I was not the "big fellow" come to do him harm. Animals are especially sensitive to the presence of Satan, and asses which run about braying loudly are believed to have seen him.

The folk do not admit to dissent or skepticism as regards their Catholic faith, despite their anti-clerical attitudes, but skepticism can be inferred from many of their utterances. Most doubt centers around the reality of the hereafter and its nature, if it exists. Invariably when I talked of religion with them, whether singly or in groups, my own views of the afterworld were solicited eagerly, and such remarks as the following, pronounced with anxiety, were forthcoming from them: "Is there really a life after death?", "Will we meet relatives there?", "Is it bodies or souls that live in Heaven?", "If we all meet in Heaven, won't it be too crowded?", "How could God be so cruel as to put people in a big fire?", and "Sure, no one has ever returned to tell of the afterlife." The most public expression of skepticism that my wife and I encountered was in a pub when she was requested to sing "Galway Bay" before a crowd of boisterous men; after she sang the line, "And if there's going to be a life hereafter," someone shouted out from the audience, "There won't be.", and the others laughed so uproariously and for so long a time that she had to discontinue singing.

Only Catholics can enter Heaven, so most islanders claim, and among the faithful only saints go directly to Heaven at death, as preordained by God. All others who escape Hell must sojourn in Purgatory, where the temporal punishment of sins previously forgiven must be endured, and the guilt of unrepented venial sins cleared away. Conceptions of Purgatory are vague, but it is felt that severe punishments are meted out there, and that the stay of most Catholics is a long one, even though mitigated by earthly indulgences and penances. Theirs is an example of what some theologians term a "dreary interpretation of Purgatory," with its emphasis on the sinful nature of man. Several times we were told that we would enter Heaven even though not Catholic, because "religions are like canoes which set out on separate courses for a mainland port, yet all reach their destination;" always we were cautioned not to disclose this personal belief to the curate.

The most significant religious events of the year in Inis Beag are certain Catholic feast days, masses performed in homes twice each year, marriages, funerals, visits to the holy well, and several pagan observances. Of the many feast days commemorating the mysteries of the faith and honoring particular saints, eight are holydays of obligation in Ireland: Circumcision, St. Patrick, Ascension, Corpus Christi, Assumption, All Saints, Immaculate Conception, and Nativity. On these days the folk attend mass, abstain from work, and do not conduct business. The feasts of St. Patrick and Christmas among these, and the lesser feasts of St. Brigid, Easter, the patron saint of Inis Beag, St. John, All Souls, St. Martin, and St. Stephen, are considered the most important locally. Although pagan elements are incorporated to some extent in all feast days, reinterpretations are most in evidence in the feasts of St. Brigid, St. John, St. Martin, and St. Stephen, and thus they will be taken up later in the chapter.

Lent in Inis Beag is a period during which men are hard at work farming, and social activities are at low ebb. The laws of fast and abstinence during Lent impose no hardships on the folk in light of the simplicity of their diet, with meat often absent from the table and only one full meal taken during the day as a matter of course. The standard of living in the island is such that for most people there is "too little to give up anything." Many islanders abstain from drinking alcoholic beverages during Lent, and will imbibe only on St. Patrick's Day, March 17th. Following the shipwreck (six days after Ash Wednesday in 1960), when salvaged Scotch whiskey was present in vast quantities, several men who had "sworn off" spirits took to drinking Vat 69 in the privacy of their homes; when the practice became known publicly, they claimed that they were "off the stout" only, which is what most men drink ordinarily because of the high cost of liquor. St. Patrick's Day is much anticipated because it is a holyday of obligation when work ceases, drink can be taken by abstainers, and there is a dance in the boat house in the evening. The dance did not materialize in 1960, because the time of flood tide, when the grounded freighter could best be boarded, coincided with the time of the dance. Before mass on St. Patrick's Day, boys in groups search for shamrocks, which, if found, will ensure the finder "riches" in the future. Women that day wear green sweaters, men shamrocks in their buttonholes, and girls green hair ribbons, and there is much visiting in the afternoon following a special meal. Women spend the last weeks of Lent preparing new clothes for their spouses, their children, and themselves, which first are worn to mass on Easter. Eggs are accumulated before the feast day so that each member of the family will have several to eat at breakfast before mass, and in some homes the children gather and hide eggs the week before Easter to see who can collect the most by Sunday morning.

June 14th in Inis Beag is "pattern day," derived from the word patron, which honors the patron saint. Until the 1920s, when suppressed by the clergy, this day and the two days following it rivaled the 12 days of Christmas in festivity. Then it was customary for people from nearby islands and the mainland to visit Inis Beag, and the local folk in turn to attend pattern days in islands and communities in their vicinity. The celebration commenced with the digging out of sand from the church of the patron saint and from his tomb, or "bed," so that during the night of vigil islanders and visitors could pray while walking around the grave and rest in the church to gain special favor from the saint and from God. The day itself saw masses celebrated in the chapel, and athletic, dancing, and other competitions staged on the strand and contiguous common land. Tents were erected to accommodate vendors of food and drink, as well as solo and figure dancers who performed to the tunes played by visiting musicians of note. Most visitors departed at the end of the day, but those who remained were invited to take part in two more days of revelry in certain island homes, where dancing, singing, and drinking prevailed day and night. It was the prevalence of factional fighting and promiscuous behavior engendered by drunkenness which prompted the church to restrict the traditional practices of pattern day.

In the 1930s, the priest inaugurated a custom of celebrating mass on pattern day in the church of the patron saint; but it persisted for only two decades, and today the bed is cleared of sand but the church is not. My wife and I observed only 11 persons praying and resting during the night of vigil in 1960. Miraculous cures, appropriately embodied in legends and anecdotes, are claimed for persons who have propitiated the patron saint in this manner in the past, and most of those who still observe the vigil are seeking relief for physical ills. The most recent cures reported are for spinal meningitis, rheumatism, a deformed knee, and an eyeball pierced with a thorn. No work is done on pattern day now, and a dance in the evening, seldom attended by visitors other than tourists, is the only vestige of the gayety which once marked the day. This dance, just as the St. Patrick's Day dance, did not take place in 1960, even though an accordionist and two other mainlanders came out by *curach* to attend it; the shyness of local girls rather than the tide was the disruptive factor on this occasion.

All Saints is a holyday of obligation November 1st, and is followed next day by another feast—All Souls. One of the most popular of humorous anecdotes deals with All Saints' Day in a neighboring island, where once long ago the Church of Ireland pastor gave the day off to men working for him; when ten days later they asked to be off once again for St. Martin's Day, he inquired with seeming pique, "And where was Martin on All Saints' Day?" The feast of All Souls is also a workless day in Inis Beag, although the cemetery is given its one cleaning of the year during the early morning. The folk visit the church and graveyard throughout the day and are awarded indulgences for their prayers in behalf of souls of the dead residing in Purgatory. In the cemetery, prayers are offered for relatives, one at a time, and then for everyone buried there, those lost at sea, and those who have no one to pray for them. An islander going to the chapel makes a succession of visits inside to pray, retiring to the churchyard after each prayer; an indulgence is granted for every visit, and some children carry small stones and pile them outside of the chapel to keep count of the indulgences thus acquired. It is said of those who remain longest in the cemetery and make the most number of visits to the chapel that they are attempting to mollify the ghosts of relatives whom they treated badly when alive.

The 12 days of Christmas commence with the feast of the Nativity on December 25th and end with the feast of the Epiphany on January 6th, and include the feasts of St. Stephen on December 26th, Holy Innocents on December 28th, and Circumcision on January 1st. This is the high point of the year for the folk, even though it is a much quieter period today than it was half a century ago, when social concerns outweighed religious ones. Work is suspended altogether on Christmas and the three days following it and on January 1st and 6th, and during the rest of the period only "light chores" are done. Importance is attached to the 12 days over and above their religious significance and the fact that little work is done; for at this time emigrants return to Inis Beag on holiday; if a marriage is to occur during the year it is likely to be arranged then; at least one party usually is given which attracts most of the adults; and the men gather in the pubs on several nights to sing, dance, and tell stories. For weeks before Christmas, rumors abound as to which relatives will visit the island, who will marry whom, and where the party will take place; these serve to sharpen the anticipation of the islanders and to make them less mindful of the worsening of the weather.

In preparation for the Christmas season, new clothes are fashioned—as at Easter—to be worn initially on the five feast days, and it is usual for a man needing a new *crios* to have it woven in time for Christmas mass. Houses and streets are cleaned and repaired, fireplaces whitewashed, and supplies are taken in for the 12 days as steamer service is curtailed. On Christmas Eve, a special dish of corned ling or cod smothered in sauce is served at "Christmas supper," and large white candles purchased in the shops are placed on the dining table and in one or more windows of the cottage, to be burned nightly during the 12 days. The sight from the sea of the darkened island with its hundreds of candles rivals in beauty the view of the mainland coast far away on St. John's Eve, when bonfires are lighted as far as the eye can see. Relatives visit one another after Christmas supper, and when the children have been put to bed, stockings are hung above the fireplace and filled by the parents with oranges, candies, ribbons, pencils, handkerchiefs, and toys for the infants. Santa Claus is the gift giver, so infants are taught, and thus he can be used to promote good behavior on their part in the weeks prior to Christmas; this belief seldom persists into childhood, however, as older children are eager to disabuse their younger siblings of it. Adults usually do not exchange gifts, but they receive them from kin and acquaintances abroad to whom they in turn send Christmas cards. On Christmas Day, special cakes and breads are served at breakfast and lamb, if available, at supper, and the family goes out only to attend mass. Many homes are decorated then for the 12 days, with cards received and sprigs of holly placed on windowsills and fireplace mantels and crepe paper and balloons hung from the ceiling. More visiting among relatives is done between St. Stephen's Day and Epiphany than at any other time of the year, and guests are treated to cakes and drinks, which include liquor.

Whereas the folk during the Christmas season are the most optimistic and expansive, they are the least so for the three or more days following the death of one of their number. Work halts until after the burial of the deceased—"out of respect for the body"—and subdued talk focuses on death and salvation and the tribulations of life on earth. It is at this time that the masochism of the islanders is most in evidence, and they are most prone to discuss the teachings of the church, to reveal doubts concerning the afterworld, and to bemoan their own sinful lives. In evaluating the career of the person who has just died, an attempt is made to explain the cause of his demise, and both natural and supernatural causes are considered. Most deaths are attributed to the natural causes of old age, illness, and accident; but death also can come as the result of God's will and the actions of the Devil and malignant pagan forces, such as witches of the evil eye and ghosts. The immediate mourning for one who dies before the age of 40 years is deep and prolonged, particularly if small children are left with only a single parent, and it is believed that "the good die young." One of the most disliked traditions in Inis Beag is that of formal mourning for a year, during which time social activities for close relatives of the deceased are curtailed severely; they cannot attend parties, sing, dance, or play music in their homes, and men must reduce in number their visits to the pubs. Life is so dull as a matter of course, so the complaint is, that placing restrictions on what few social activities are available makes it almost unbearable.

When a person dies, his body is "waked" in the house until taken in procession to the church during the late afternoon of the day following death. Another procession escorts the coffin to the cemetery early the next morning, after it has stood the night unattended near the altar. How many folk attend the wake and compose the two processions depends on the number of the dead person's kin, his prestige status, and how well he was liked. The "laying out" of the corpse for the wake is done by close female relatives of the deceased; they wash the body and powder its face, put on the clothes or habit, and prepare the bed on which the corpse will rest. A man may be attired in new white bawneens and *crios* and a woman in her wedding dress, but it is becoming more common today for the body to be clothed in a purchased brown habit. On the breast the hands are crossed and rosary beads entwined in the fingers, and the corpse is covered up to the chest with a white sheet which later is used to wrap it up in the coffin. The manufacture of the coffin usually is assigned to one of the canoe and furniture makers, who assembles it crudely with unpainted boards and delivers it the night of the wake or the following morning.

The wake now is a solemn occasion in most of Ireland, and is attended for the purpose of praying for the soul of the dead and sympathizing with the relatives of the deceased. But until recently it was a gay affair, merrier than a wedding, characterized by storytelling, games of various sorts, contests of strength, taunting and mocking, mischief-making, and factional fighting (O Suilleabhain 1967: 26–129). It is hard to imagine a wake more somber than that which takes place in Inis Beag. Most of those who attend it do so before midnight and stay two to three hours, coming and going at will, while "only those who own him stay all night." Each visitor on arrival prays briefly at the bedside of the deceased or in the doorway of the room before expressing condolences, and at midnight all who are anywhere in the wake-house kneel and recite the responses of the Rosary intoned by the curate. Immediate kin express their grief in muffled sobs beside the corpse, but the ancient wailing lament for the dead, known as the "keen," no longer is heard in Inis Beag. Tables and benches are set up in the kitchen on which the men sit silently or converse in whispers with their neighbors, as they drink stout or whiskey and pass around clay pipes offered them "to keep the night awake." Most of the women congregate in the room of the dead, where only very old women smoke pipes. I have counted as many as 18 minutes of absolute silence at a wake and have never heard laughter.

Before the procession to the church forms, men tend to gather in small groups outside the house of the deceased and women gather inside the house. After the corpse is placed in the coffin, close relatives and even friends shake the hand and kiss the face of the dead person before the top is nailed down; then the box is carried to the front street and placed across two chairs for prayers to be said and holy water sprinkled over it by the priest. A white sheet is draped on the casket, and six pallbearers shoulder it and carry it through a gap made in the stone fence to the road which leads to the chapel. The pallbearers are both agnatic and uterine kin of the deceased, excluding his sons, and two of them have the further duty of digging the shallow grave that night or in the morning before the body is interred. Moving slowly behind the coffin bearers, the procession is headed by the spouse and sons of the dead person, followed by his daughters, then women, and finally men in a long, slow moving, silent column; children other than the offspring of the deceased seldom join the procession, and the sexes walk separately. The curate may or may not lead this procession and the one the next morning, sometimes preferring to go ahead to church and cemetery by himself. A son of the dead person treats the grave diggers to stout in a pub before they set out with spades for the graveyard, as he does the pallbearers after they return from the church. In the past, the grave was dug as part of the funeral service, but this custom was altered as the cemetery became filled and occasionally diggers by accident broke into previously interred coffins revealing their contents. A number of grisly legends and anecdotes tell of islanders buried alive by mistake, or whose bodies were partially preserved, as revealed by such accidents.

The procession from the chapel to the graveyard leaves the modern road, as we saw in Chapter 1, to follow an ancient, obliterated trail past a church believed to have been buried beneath the sand centuries ago, and then climbs the long hill of kitchen midden and sand to the gate of the cemetery. Here the column breaks up, some people going to the graves of relatives to pray and others to the newly opened grave. Men and women kneel separately at the graveside for the service (see Fig. 11), and many of the women cry as the casket is lowered into the shallow

Figure 11. Praying at the graveside of an islander

grave by the two diggers who have leaped into the hole. After the priest has thrown three shovelfuls of dirt on the coffin, the grave is filled in rapidly by the diggers, and the close kin of the deceased and the pallbearers gather around the priest to recite a final Rosary. Those who did not visit the graves of relatives when entering the cemetery do so as they depart. Some graves remain unmarked following the funeral; others are marked with a wooden cross or uninscribed slab of local limestone; while still others have placed over them engraved headstones purchased on the mainland. Several large, flat tombstones dating back over a century cover members of particular families buried atop one another as sand accumulated.

Twice a year, Inis Beag is visited for a day by the parish priest and a curate, who join the local curate to celebrate special masses, called "the stations" ("the confessions" in Irish), in two homes and in the church. Homes are chosen in such a manner that each of the four villages is represented every year, and each home in the island is so honored every 16 to 22 years. For weeks in advance of the stations, both families are hard at work cleaning, painting, and repairing their houses and surrounding streets, fences, and outbuildings in preparation for the event. Confessions are heard by the three priests the night before, and holy water is sprinkled by them in the streets and on the outbuildings near the two houses as a blessing prior to the masses at nine o'clock in the morning. Stations in the homes are conducted by the visiting clerics and in the chapel by the Inis Beag curate, and the folk are free to attend any one of the three services. Following the masses, the priests and the three local teachers are entertained at breakfast in the chosen homes, after which the sacrament is carried to those who are confined. The families involved look forward eagerly to the event, for the stations are believed to bring them luck and "to drive out the 'big fellow' for a long time." It also forces them to put their property in a state of good repair, which, in retrospect, is regarded as a benefit, however much they might have complained of the labor involved during the previous weeks.

The sacred well, probably appropriated from the Druids 13 centuries ago, still attracts the folk and occasionally pilgrims from Inis Thiar and other islands. On the mainland, patterns often were associated with holy wells named after saints, but this does not seem to have been the case in Inis Beag. It was customary until about ten years ago for those who came to pray here to attach bits of cloth, rosaries, or sacred objects obtained from holy places of pilgrimage on the mainland and abroad, but this practice was halted by the clergy as smacking of paganism. Now it is visited for religious purposes mostly by small groups on Sunday afternoon, and by persons about to emigrate and their families who come to pray for the good fortune of the soon departed. The water in the spring is not considered holy, but capable of "bringing the grace of God and the saint," and if it is drunk during prayer, it is believed to be especially efficacious for curing sterility, among other afflictions. In this century, a partially blind islander is believed to have regained his sight after paying nine visits to the well on successive Sundays, and other miraculous cures from earlier times are reported. Those who come to the spring always seek a tiny fish or eel in the water, which, if observed, is merely a good omen to some but an assurance of reaching Heaven to others. Attaching rags to the well and seeking cures and omens there are all examples of reinterpretation. The spring also is used as a source of water by farmers who pasture stock in nearby fields and by thirsting passersby.

Pagan Supernaturalism

Pagan supernaturalism is disavowed by the folk, and it is difficult to know how widely held are beliefs in this sphere. That they are held is indisputable, as attested by the active efforts of curates up to this day to eradicate them. Youth of the island overtly deny the existence of other than church approved spiritual entities, although the most outspoken disclaimer of paganism among them is visited occasionally by the ghost of his father, who urges the continuation of a family feud. But elders cling tenaciously to indigenous beliefs and practices, about which they are extremely secretive for fear of being ridiculed by outsiders and their more skeptical fellows. Defensive about being labeled backward, the islanders feel that the "superstitions" they are said to hold most contribute to this impression. When the folk talk of pagan retentions and reinterpretations, they ascribe them to those who lived at the time that their parents or grandparents did, or to certain of their superstitious contemporaries. A notorious dissenter, who sometimes has occasion to patrol the shores of Inis Beag before dawn, antagonizes his neighbors by deriding them for their fear of venturing after dark to the back of the island, where fairies and ghosts hold sway. On telling him of my intention to spend a night resting atop a *clochán* near the Atlantic coast, he said, "The only thing that will happen is you'll hear the cocks crow in the morning." He is the only person who admitted to me that he disbelieves the teachings of the church concerning the soul and its fate. In further mocking his fellows for their apprehensions about death and its aftermath, he proclaimed that the soul, "if there is such a thing, goes nowhere after the heart stops beating."

Celtic deities no longer are a part of the belief system of the islanders, but the culture heroes of the Iron Age—such as Cuchulainn, Finn, and Oisin—still are extolled in legends, and the promontory fort and other ancient monuments and some of the geographical features (for instance, glacial boulders) in Inis Beag and nearby islands are explained by the actions of Celtic heroes. Spirits, demons, and witches of many sorts are the supernatural beings from the Celtic, and possibly pre-Celtic, era which figure most importantly in the pagan segment of the folk religion. They have become incorporated into orthodox Catholicism by being declared "works of the Devil" by those who admit to their existence (It is said that two priests of peasant background have admitted to this belief publicly in Inis Beag.)—a reinterpretation resorted to by many primitive and folk peoples under the duress of acculturation with dominance. The spiritual entities most linked with the Irish, both in writings and in popular imagination, are the trooping and solitary fairies, known to the islanders as the "little people," "good people," or "gentry." In Inis Beag, only the leprechaun and "red man" among the numerous solitary fairies are known. William Butler Yeats numbers the banshee, mermaid, pookah, and water horse among the solitary fairies (Yeats ND :76–77), but these are not regarded as such by the folk (The latter two are animal spirits, or demons, rather than human spirits.); also found in Inis Beag are the sea spirit, or "headless body," and other minor spirits and demons.

Fairies seldom permit themselves to be seen, but most of the islanders have experienced their presence, if only through having objects mysteriously misplaced by them or hearing them sing and cobble. These beings differ considerably in appearance—according to type, sex, and age—but most of them are knee-high and wear green jackets, flat red caps, and buckled shoes. The trooping fairies live in clochán and thorn bushes and spend most of their time feasting, singing, dancing, fighting, playing games, and making love. A spirited hurling match played by fairies on the strand was described to me by an observer who had witnessed it from a canoe approaching the island; he and his mates rowed close enough to overhear the creatures call out to each other by name. Small whirlwinds are a sign of their passing, and a farmer who was haying and failed to say the proper "God bless them.", as such a wind stirred his field, was punished by having all of the cocks that he had accumulated blown away. One verse of my ballad, poorly received by most islanders, tells of men who were afraid to board the freighter for several nights after trooping fairies had been seen dining in the mess and a ghost pacing the deck. Fairies disregard human beings most of the time, but they can harm those who disregard or speak ill of them, as well as play "fairy pranks" out of sheer capriciousness. One of their favorite modes of attack is to cast "fairy darts" at their victims; on the mainland, these are prehistoric flint artifacts, but in Inis Beag they are any small pebbles supposedly thrown from the sky to cause bodily harm. An Inis Thiar man collected a number of darts allegedly cast at him by irate gentry, only to have the collection confiscated by the curate in whom he indiscreetly confided. The most feared practice of trooping fairies is that of stealing souls of children and leaving in their place changelings, who gradually sicken and die. Since boys are favored over girls, Irish peasants of the region until recently dressed their male offspring in petticoats, sometimes up to the age of 18 years, to deceive the little people. Even now parents are loath to praise the health or beauty of their children for fear that the gentry will overhear and be prompted to victimize their souls.

Solitary fairies are described by Yeats as "withered, old, and solitary, in every way unlike the sociable [trooping fairies]. . . . They dress with all unfairy homeliness, and are, indeed, most sluttish, slouching, peering, mischievous phantoms" (Yeats ND :76). The long occupation of Inis Beag by leprechauns is evidenced by the Garden of the Cobbler and a spring at the back of the island, shaped like the sole of a shoe, which is known as Well of the Boot. Occasionally a leprechaun has been seen in the former location, but only the sound of a tapping hammer has been heard in the latter. Instead of guarding a buried pot of gold at the foot of a rainbow, as popularly conceived, the leprechaun of Inis Beag possesses a small purse in which he keeps but a single coin. Children sometimes are urged to hunt for the hidden purse, as a distraction by harassed parents. The rift valley between Castle and High Villages is thought to be the home of at least one "red man." He wears a pointed cap to denote cleverness and has a laugh, as distinctive as the hammering of the leprechaun, by which his presence is known. A practical joker with poltergeist qualities, the red man prefers to frequent houses, where his mischief is countered with bottles of holy water. From November of 1959 until June of 1963, my wife and I experienced, first in Inis Beag and then in our home in the United States, the antics of an unseen being who opened doors and windows, turned on lights and water faucets, and imbibed our Irish whiskey. Tongue-in-cheek, we placed the blame for these uncanny occurrences on an amiable solitary fairy who had attached himself to us, but eventually I felt compelled to report our unique contact with the Celtic supernatural to the anthropological community—a gesture regarded as "poison oak in the scientific groves of academe" (Messenger 1962:367–373).

The spiritual omens of death are three in Inis Beag: the sound of trooping fairies building a coffin for the victim, soft tapping on the window pane of his bedroom, and the wailing of the banshee during the night before his demise. No one has ever viewed the banshee, but many have heard her cry out in the night, and the keen of Celtic derivation is said to be an imitation of her funeral call. She attaches herself only to certain families which inherit her patrilineally. An aged Inis Beag man was seriously ill with influenza on the night that my wife and I sponsored a dancing party, and a young man departing from it three hours after midnight played his accordion as he walked to his home located near that of the sick person. On learning of this event, the nurse shortly after dawn hurried to her patient to assure him that the wails he might have heard came from the instrument of the inexpert youth and not from the family banshee; at this news, thanatomania was prevented and the man lived another three weeks, when the banshee at last cried and was heard by those at his deathbed. Opinion is divided as to whether it is the fairies or the banshee who announce death by window tapping, but as a practical joke islanders long ago used to tap on the bedroom windows of those persons considered overly superstitious. Interesting to note here is the fact that even before the beginning of this century, strength of belief in the pagan supernatural varied among the folk.

Three water dwellers found in the ocean surrounding Inis Beag are the mermaid, sea spirit, and water horse. At least one and maybe three mermaids are associated with particular locations along the coastline of the island. This spirit usually is found sitting on a rock with her fish tail in the water and combing her long hair, although she has been seen hovering over the surface of the sea in a "robe of mist." Discussion of her in the pubs always induces embarrassment among the men, because her perfectly formed female upper body is nude and not always hidden by her tresses; she appears to delight in exposing herself to the puritanical folk. The sea spirit is called the "headless body" for the reason that his seaweed covered hulk lacks any appendages. Like the seal who bears a human soul, he favors following in the wake of *curach*—bobbing up and down in the water and staring balefully at the seamen with huge eyes. Only by dropping an object containing gold into the ocean deeps, which the spirit finds irresistible, can his pursuit be impeded short of rowing back to the island. My wife and I brought to Inis Beag a foot-high statue of a troll, purchased two years before in Norway, made of moss with large glass eyes, which we hung from the wall of our kitchen (as we had from the dashboard of our car) as a good luck charm. It aroused excitement among fishermen who visited us because of its resemblance to the headless body; one man reasoned that this being must inhabit all of the northern seas, and probably arouses equal consternation among Scottish and Scandinavian seafarers. The water horse is a demon counterpart of the mermaid, with black body of a steed and tail of a giant fish. Until 40 years ago, it lived in the fresh water lake of Inis Beag, where it was seen on certain nights traveling abreast the surface with its head held high and mane waving in the wind. Now it is seen only at sea and infrequently at great distance.

The single pookah of Inis Beag resides in a Copper-Bronze Age tumulus (see Fig. 12), which became a medieval cemetery with rough headstones still in place; located on the western margin of the common land, it is known as the Hill of Ferns. In the Middle Ages, the church urged systematic reinterpretation of Christian and pagan elements (It was advocated as early as 601 by Pope Gregory VII in a letter to priests who were proselytizing the primitive Britons.). This policy is attested in Inis Beag and neighboring islands not only by Christian graveyards being located contiguous to pagan ones, but by Christian church buildings incorporating Druidic temples and Celtic holy wells being appropriated by Christian worshippers. During the day, the "dog of the tumulus," as this demon is called, will twist the limbs of unwary individuals who chance to fall asleep on the mound, and at night it is known to race across the sands of strand and common land, altering its size at will from that of a small dog to that of a bull, to frighten those who might be passing. It appears that Irish emigrants carried both the mermaid and pookah abroad with them as early as the seventeenth century, at least to the West Indies. In doing research among the "Black Irish" of Montserrat during 1965, 1966, and last year, I discovered a mermaid with white skin who guards a pot of gold buried on top of Chance's Mountain, and a pookah in the form of a

Figure 12. Copper-Bronze Age tumulus—home of the pookah

black dog which roams the road by the Catholic church and cemetery in the village of St. Patrick, altering its size instantaneously (Messenger 1967:37–38).

Witchcraft once flourished in Inis Beag, so it is held, but today only the casting of the evil eye still is practiced. The most common witch of the past was an ugly old woman, called a "hag witch," who was native to Inis Beag or a transient nighttime intruder from nearby islands and the mainland. She was able to fly through the air swiftly, make herself invisible, assume any size or shape, enter the body of an animal, and perpetrate black magic. Her favorite animal familiar was the rabbit and her favorite target the cow, whose milk she purloined after midnight from beasts pastured at the back of the island. Like the trooping fairies, she too stole the souls of children and left ailing changelings in their stead. When it was suspected by parents that a child was a changeling rather than their human offspring, it was customary to throw it into the fireplace or burn the bedding on which it lay in order to retrieve the departed soul; if the perpetrator were a witch, she would leap from the flames with a "wild shriek" and vanish, leaving the restored child in perfect health in her place. I was told in Inis Thiar of islanders there who bear scars from being burned when their souls were rescued by this expediency.

Three Inis Beag persons are accused of possessing the evil eye and thus are shunned by their fellows. Such a witch is known by a disfigurement in or near his left eye, from which the malignant force emanates, and by his ability to cause misfortune to those whom he compliments. The extent of his power is measured by how soon after the compliment his victim suffers, and how serious is the calamity. Most feared of recent witches is a man who as a youth caused a newly arrived curate on his first walk of the island to fall and break his leg; within seconds after the boy praised the vigorous stride of the priest, "the poor creature disappeared behind a fence, feet over head." The folk seldom compliment one another, and when they do they append "God bless you." to the statement as a precautionary incantation. Persons with the evil eye neglect to do this, it is said. I often have wondered—when in a mood to credit the existence of fairies which turn on water faucets in the dead of night—if a series of misfortunes which befell me during 1960 and 1961 was somehow linked to one of these persons wishing me a good year, without uttering "God bless you.", as my wife and I put off the strand in a canoe at the end of our research. The same incantation is voiced by those in the vicinity of one who sneezes—in this case to prevent his soul from being captured by the fairies. It is tempting to attribute the unwillingness of Irish peasants generally to pay compliments to the age-old but now forgotten dread of being accused of the evil eye and of inviting fairies and hag witches to substitute changelings for human children.

Priests of the church at least a century ago rid Inis Beag of most religious practitioners of pagan disposition, but there is evidence that before their acculturative influence was felt diviners and workers of good and evil magic practiced techniques which had their roots in the Iron Age. Divining now is restricted mostly to the seeking of omens by everyone, and the astrological and tea leaf reading skills of several persons who do not charge for their services. The principal workers of magic in the past were herbalists, animal doctors, and bone setters; an animal doctor in Inis Beag and a bone setter in a nearby island still ply their inherited specialties for pay, but both men claim that they are practical folk physicians and do not command pagan or Christian spiritual powers. Just as the islanders share a common body of omens which are used to avoid the misfortunes and compound the benefits in store for them, they also share a common knowledge of folk medicines, which some believe to be more efficacious than the medicines provided by doctor and nurse. Indigenous medicines once were prescribed by workers of magic, misnamed "herb witches"—old women who gathered plants at dawn and "brewed" them in a variety of ways to affect various cures. The dew on the plants, as well as the manner in which they were compounded, gave these medicines a magical potency. To meet such a witch as she was returning from collecting ingredients meant that one was doomed to take on the affliction of the patient being treated by the hag. A similar belief, well represented in the folklore of the islanders, is the transference of disease from a human being to an animal that he has befriended earlier.

Christian and Pagan Reinterpretations

The four quarterly festivals of the Celts were: Imbolc, celebrated on February 1st, Beltaine on May 1st, Lughnasa on August 1st, and Samhain on

November 1st. Imbolc heralded the coming of spring with the lactation of ewes, while at Beltaine cattle were driven to open grazing after passing between bonfires which magically protected them against disease and ensured their fertility. The harvest commenced with Lughnasa, and the grazing season ended with Samhain. Of these festivals, Imbolc has become reinterpreted with the feast of St. Brigid; Beltaine and Samhain, known today as May Day and Allhallows respectively, have remained almost untouched by Christianity and are observed in Inis Beag; but Lughnasa has disappeared from island tradition. Lughnasa still is celebrated in many parts of Ireland and is the subject of a monumental folklore study—Maire MacNeill's *The Festival of Lughnasa*; until the introduction of early potatoes into Inis Beag, harvesting commenced on this day, but any other practices associated with Lughnasa were abandoned long ago. Minor pagan festivals have become reinterpreted with Whitsuntide and the feasts of St. John, St. Martin, and St. Stephen, all of which are observed in Inis Beag.

Brigid, the most renowned of Irish female saints, was a cowherd and therefore is associated with cattle and with flowers, such as the dandelion, which nourish young lambs in the spring. On the last day of January, a small "Brigid's Cross" is fashioned from straw in each household of Inis Beag, and is thrust into the thatching at the end of the feast day. Crosses once were made from rushes, wood, metal, and even paper, and it is possible to determine the age of a thatched cottage being dismantled or renovated by counting the number of crosses salvaged from the straw debris. The Celts worshipped the sun whose symbol was the swastika, and the Brigid's Cross takes this form. It is a charm which protects the house (and the byre on the mainland) and those within it from harm, especially by fire, during the year. At the beginning of this century, a destitute woman who lived alone used to go from door to door begging for food and carrying a large "Brigid's Doll" made of straw and dressed immaculately in white with a picture of the saint on its breast. Some of the folk pulled straw from the doll to manufacture their crosses. After the woman recited the following poem, she was presented with food in honor of the saint, for which she blessed each person in the household with the doll:

> Here comes Brigid   She is deaf and
> Dressed in white.   She is dumb.
> Give her something   For God's sake,
> For the night.   Give her some.

Today, small groups of girls travel about the island emulating their predecessor by begging for coins to buy candy and donate to the church. A Brigid's Doll dressed in confirmation garb is carried by the leader of each group, and is used to confer blessings after the girls have recited in unison the two verses.

May Eve and Allhallows' Eve are both times when it is dangerous to go out of doors alone at night or be abroad after midnight, for the "big fellow" roams the back of the island, and everywhere pagan fairies, witches, vindictive ghosts, and the dog of the tumulus search for human victims. The safety of cattle is of particular concern to the folk on May Eve, and a common practice is to attach to the horn or tail of a cow a cloth containing a piece of iron which has been blessed, to protect the beast from milk pilfering fairies and hag witches. Among the taboos associated with May Day are those prohibiting the visiting of wells before dawn and giving away fire; as regards the latter taboo, to do so is to "give away the luck of the farm" for a year. Flowers are placed on the altars of the two medieval churches in the early morning of May Day, and at one time garlands of flowers shaped like a horseshoe were hung on door posts for luck. Souls of the dead are especially feared on Allhallows' Eve, and are placated in the Catholic tradition a day later on the feast of All Souls. The telling of stories is tabooed on Allhallows' Day, and the fairies are said to spoil wild blackberries for future eating with their before dawn depredations. My wife and I invited in a small group of islanders to celebrate Halloween in 1959, and we spent much of the evening having our fortunes told by an old man as it was done on this night when he was a youth; he poured melted lead through a key handle into a pan of cold water and made his prognostications by interpreting the configurations formed by the quick hardening metal.

Whitsuntide is the week beginning with the feast of Pentecost, or Whit-sunday, but in Inis Beag it extends to the feast of Corpus Christi and is known as the "kinkish time," when once again evil forces hold sway in the island. Usually the weather is "heavy and close" and very changeable, I was told, and people tend to be irritable and more depressed than usual. Men do not cut their hair, nor does anyone wash themselves, during these 12 days. Although the pookah is always a danger, it is more active at this time than during the rest of the year, and children and visitors are warned not to fall asleep outside or even to sit down on the ground unless accompanied by others, whose presence will thwart any attempts by the demon to twist their limbs. Some islanders will not undertake major tasks or decide on important issues during Whitsuntide. Whereas Christmas and Easter are considered "lucky times," the "kinkish time" is unlucky, and those born then may have the evil eye or be destined to die violently or take a life.

In 1960, Corpus Christi was celebrated June 16th—two days after pattern day and eight days before St. John's Eve. The latter is one of several midsummer celebrations reported from Ireland which mark the summer solstice. Boys gather wood and tend a huge bonfire lighted just after sunset on the common land of Inis Beag, and a few islanders carry coals from it to their homes and fields for protection and to guarantee the fertility of their wives and female livestock. A man complained to me that an infection in his son's finger was caused by the failure of the boy to procure a coal from the fire as instructed. On that evening, the folk congregate outside of their cottages and along the terrace roads to watch the hundreds of bonfires alight on the mainland coast. In the past, cows were driven between twin bonfires as at Beltaine, and barren women and those yet to marry leaped over the dying flames. One of the most brilliant satirical novels of Irish life—both cruel and insightful—is Tracy's *The Straight and Narrow Path*, the plot of which focuses on the difficulties encountered by a vacationing British anthropologist after he writes for a newspaper an eye witness account of nuns jumping a St. John's Eve bonfire.

The legends are several and varied in Ireland about the life of St. Martin (O Suilleabhain 1957:252–261). There is no saint of this name who is of Irish origin, and the church honors St. Martin of Tours in the liturgy of November 11th. O Suilleabhain suggests that the Catholic feast has been reinterpreted with a pagan festival, which had the sacrificial shedding of blood as one of its main facets. St. Martin also is associated with the grinding of corn and with miraculous powers for causing growth in plants and creating animals from inanimate matter. In Inis Beag, the saint is regarded as a miller who was martyred in Ireland during the Middle Ages by being cast under a mill wheel and ground to death. A few islanders still observe the taboos of not turning wheels or spinning on the vigil and feast day to honor his martyrdom. The Sunday before St. Martin's Day is called "bloody Sunday," when those who can afford to do so butcher a sheep to be consumed by the family on the feast day; others less fortunate kill a fowl or duck during the vigil. Using the sacrificed animal's blood, the father or mother makes the sign of the cross on the forehead of each member of the family, while praying that the saint guard the safety of all in the year to follow. Some folk use the blood to bless in a like manner the fireplace, bedposts, front door, and outbuildings; all crosses, including those on the forehead, are allowed to remain until obliterated by natural causes.

Just as the girls of Inis Beag carry the Brigid's Doll and beg from door to door on the feast day of the saint, the boys do the same with a wren attached to a long wooden pole on the morning of St. Stephen's Day, the feast day following Christmas. The "wrenboys" travel in pairs and are invited into each home, where they are awarded coins for dancing and singing this song:

> Wren, wren, the king of the birds,
> St. Stephen's Day he was caught in the furze.
> So little I am, my family is great.
> Get up landlady and give us a break.
>
> Up with the kettle and down with the pan,
> And give us a shilling to carry the wren.
> If you haven't a shilling a ha'penny will do.
> If you haven't a ha'penny—God bless you.

Handkerchiefs, ribbons, and a sprig of holly also are attached to the pole, and in 1959 only one pair of youths managed to "hunt the wren" successfully and thus maintain the tradition. A home is not blessed by these visitations, as in the case of the groups of girls on St. Brigid's Day, but the act of giving money is believed to bring luck to the household. In some regions of the mainland, wrenboys wear straw masks, animal skins, or horns, and carry the wren on a holly bush or decorated wooden tray as they march in procession shouting and singing songs to the accompaniment of homemade skin tambourines (Evans 1957:279). Little is known of the pagan roots of the ceremony.

In addition to the reinterpretations associated with the holy well and with Celtic festivals, there are many others of lesser significance of which only three will be considered here: beliefs concerning ghosts, the evil eye, and the afterworld. We have seen that most of the folk have had contact of some sort with the fairies; they also have witnessed ghosts—called "shades"—in corporeal form in Inis Beag or sailing the surrounding waters. These beings, who "aren't of this world," sometimes are recognized as recently deceased islanders, but more often they are "strangers" from another generation or another region of Ireland. They appear and disappear without warning and travel silently singly or in small groups. Usually they pay little or no heed to the living who chance to observe them, but they will attack those who have wronged them and occasionally others for seemingly no reason. A man told me of being beaten severely by three unknown men, obviously shades, early one evening at the back of the island; he might have been killed but for the intervention of two women, also strangers to him. At one time, persons who feared being assaulted by vengeful or capricious ghosts carried coals to protect themselves. The folk believe that shades are souls of the dead in Purgatory, which embraces the earth as well as a spiritual locus. While on earth, they do penance by laboring at economic tasks—carrying seaweed, planting gardens, and fishing—near their former homes, and the work that they accomplish is undone once they disappear.

Christianity touches on the evil eye in more ways than providing the magical incantation, "God bless you.", which automatically opposes the power of God to that of the witch. Many islanders explain the evil eye by positing the presence of both the deity and the Devil in each human body. God rests on the right side and urges a person to do good deeds, while Satan rests on the left and tempts him to commit sins. In most individuals, the deity dominates the body much of the time, but in the case of one with the evil eye, the Devil somehow has gained perpetual ascendancy and transmits his destructive power through the left eye of the person. It is the constant flowing of malignant power from within which causes the disfigurement in or near the left eye of the witch. The association of evil with the left is a phenomenon widely distributed among the peoples of the world, as is the linking of evil with black. Ghost masks are painted black to symbolize their evil nature by the Anang of Nigeria, and sacrifices to deity and ancestors at shrines are made with the right hand, and to ghosts, witches, and the spirit of sorcery with the left. In Inis Beag, people who have swarthy skin, black hair, and brown eyes, although not considered witches, are thought to possess evil power of some sort and are to be avoided. A curate possessing these physical traits who served in the island recently was mistrusted and shunned whenever possible even though "a man chosen by God Almighty." An interesting conjecture is how successful would be the research in Inis Beag of an anthropologist with dark complexion and hair and a cast in his brown left eye.

The afterworld of the Celts, known as the Isle of the Blest or the Land of Youth, lay to the west of Ireland. It has been sighted by a few fortunate Inis Beag fishermen, either low-lying on the horizon with lights sparkling when it has risen from the sea, as it does periodically, or in the ocean deeps with the spires of its buildings and their tolling bells near the surface. This is a forested land inhabited by souls of the dead, and by fairies who travel to and from the mainland in "fairy ships." Few islanders now syncretize the Isle of the Blest with the Christian Heaven, as was common a century ago, but there are those who claim to have seen fairy ships from there skirt Inis Beag headed for the mainland. These are masted schooners carrying lights with no signs of life on their decks, which heave into sight and vanish instantaneously and can move far more swiftly than their counterparts fashioned by human hands. A valley in Inis Thiar is believed to have been created by such a ship passing over the island, "with a great roar and blowing of wind." According to Celtic tradition, souls not only transmigrated to the Land of Youth but became reincarnated on earth or embodied in animals through metempsychosis. The belief in reincarnation appears not to have persisted in Inis Beag, but seals sometimes are thought to be repositories of souls; those creatures so possessed look and act human and attach themselves to fishermen who have aided or harmed them, and whose *curach* they will pursue relentlessly. I was told by an old man of a seal that he had cursed at sea for fouling his net, which later followed in his wake for many miles glaring with rage, and finally pursued him 30 feet onto the strand as he and his frightened mates carried the canoe hurriedly to its cot.

Religion and Personality

It is appropriate here to assess the basic personality structure of Inis Beag islanders, since traits such as sexual puritanism, hypochondria, depression, masochism, conformism, and ambivalence toward authority are linked causally with religion in a very direct manner. Other personality characteristics, already or yet to be considered, which are more peripheral to religion include secretiveness, envy and jealousy, dogmatism, indolence, feelings of inferiority, and verbal skill.

Probably the most prominent trait of Inis Beag (and Irish) personality is sexual puritanism. Its etiology is complex and much debated, but appears to embrace most significantly historical (such as the influence of ascetic monasticism and Jansenism), sociocultural (such as the Oedipus complex and male solidarity), and psychological (such as masochism) variables. How long it has been a major component of Irish national character is conjectural, for it is impossible to appraise with accuracy Irish society, culture, and personality prior to the nineteenth century. Sexual attitudes and behavior in Celtic, medieval, and early modern times can be surmised only from tangential and questionable sources; depending on which sources are quoted, as good a case can be made for sexual puritanism as its opposite before 1800.

The inculcation of sexual puritanism in Inis Beag must be examined in three contexts: informal social controls of the curate and those imposed by the islanders on themselves, the influence of visiting "missions," and enculturation in the home. The first of these has been taken up at length in the last chapter. Suffice it to say here, some folk (especially certain youths who consider themselves "worldly") resent the intrusions of priests and neighbors into their sexual lives. They ask what right have young, virginal, inexperienced, and sexually unknowledgeable curates to give advice and pass judgments in this sphere. Equally resented are those persons who hide themselves in the darkness or behind fences to overhear the conversations of passersby, which may pertain to sexual matters, and those who maintain close scrutiny of visitors during the summer, both day and night, in order to discover them in "compromising" situations. Sexual rumors run rife in the island, such as those concerning the "nude" sunbathing of mainland girls (bared shoulders and lower thighs) and the "attacks" on them at night by boys and young men (attempts to hold their hands or kiss them, while under the influence of stout). Over a dozen efforts on the part of my wife and me to determine the truth behind the most pernicious rumors of this genre revealed sexual phantasy at their core in every case.

Church influence also is exerted through missions which come to Inis Beag every three to five years. On these momentous occasions, two Redemptorist priests (usually, but also Franciscans, Dominicans, and Passionists) spend a week in the island, where they conduct mass each morning and preach long sermons in the chapel every afternoon or early evening. Everyone—even old people and mothers with newborn infants—is urged to attend to receive the "blessings of the mission;" to some this means gaining time out of Purgatory for themselves or a deceased kinsman, while to others absence carries with it the penalty of damnation. A mission usually has a theme whose variations are explored with high emotion and eloquence by the visiting priests in their exhortations. The most common theme is "controlling one's passions," but abstaining from intoxicating drink and maintaining the faith as an emigrant also are addressed. Collections are made by children to support the endeavor, and a list of contributors and their donations is displayed publicly. It is said that a mission creates an emotionally charged atmosphere in the island which continues for weeks after the departure of the clerics.

The seeds of repression are planted early in infancy by parents through instruction supplemented by rewards and punishments, conscious imitation, and unconscious internalization. Although mothers bestow considerable attention and affection on their offspring, particularly on their sons, physical love as manifested in intimate fondling and kissing is rare in Inis Beag. Verbal affection comes to supplant contact affection by the time that the child can walk. Any forms of direct or indirect sexual expression—masturbation, mutual exploration of bodies, use of either standard or slang words relating to sex, and open urination and defecation—are punished severely by word and deed. Care is taken to cover the bodies of infants in the presence of their siblings and outsiders, and sex never is discussed before children of any age. Separation of the sexes starts within the family among siblings in early childhood, and is augmented by separation in almost all segments of adolescent and adult activity. Brothers come to associate mostly with brothers, and sisters with sisters, at play in and near the cottage, traveling to and from school, and in the chapel. Boys and girls are separated to some extent in classrooms and completely in play at recess. During church services, there is a further separation of adult men and women, as well as boys and girls, and each of the four groups leaves the chapel in its turn. Even on the strand during summer months, male tourists and vacationing emigrants tend to bathe at one end and women at the other; some swimmers change into bathing suits there, under towels and dresses "daringly"—a custom practiced elsewhere in Ireland which bespeaks of sexual catharsis.

Parents and their school age offspring read the popular religious journals found in most homes, and many of the articles therein deal with sexual morality of the Irish Catholic variety. Several times my wife inadvertently inquired as to whether or not certain women were pregnant, using that word before children, only to be "hushed" or to have the conversations postponed until the young people could be herded outside; even then the adults were so embarrassed by the term that they found it difficult to communicate with her. One steamer day she aroused stupefaction among a group of men on the strand when she tried—unsuccessfully—to identify the gender of a bullock about to be shipped off.

Lack of sexual knowledge and the prevalence of misconceptions about sex combine to brand Inis Beag one of the most sexually naive of the world's societies. Only three mothers admitted giving sexual instructions, briefly and incompletely, to their daughters. It is said that boys are better advised than girls, but that the former learn about sex informally from older boys and men, and from observing animals covertly. Most islanders who were questioned about how sexual knowledge is imparted to youths expressed the belief that "after marriage, nature takes its course," thus negating the need for anxiety creating confrontations of parents and offspring. I was unable to discover any cases of childlessness in Inis Beag based on sexual ignorance of spouses, as have been reported from other regions of peasant Ireland.

Menstruation and the menopause arouse profound misgivings among women of the island, because few of them comprehend their physiological significance. My wife was called on by perplexed women to explain these processes more than any other phenomena related to sex. When they reach puberty, most girls are unprepared for the first menstrual flow and find the experience a traumatic one, especially when their mothers are unwilling or unable to explain it satisfactorily. It is commonly believed that the menopause can induce insanity; in order to ward it off, some women have retired from life in their mid-forties and, in at least three contemporary cases, have confined themselves to bed until death years later. Yet the harbingers of "madness" are simply the physical symptoms announcing the menopause, which in Inis Beag include migraine headaches, hot flashes, faintness in crowds and enclosed places, and severe anxiety. Sometimes women who have not yet reached the menopause or have passed it and who fear becoming mentally ill from other causes will experience these symptoms in their anticipatory role playing.

As to sexual misconceptions, the folk share with most Western peoples the belief that men by nature are far more sexually disposed than women. The latter are informed by the curate and in the home that sexual relations with their husbands are a "duty" which must be "endured," for to refuse coitus is a mortal sin. Women frequently affix the guilt for male libidinal strivings on the enormous intake of potatoes by their spouses (Among the Anang of Nigeria, men fear the excessive sexual demands of their wives and place the blame on clitoridectomy.). Asked to compare the sexual proclivities of Inis Beag men and women, one woman said, "Men can wait a long time for 'it,' but we can wait a lot longer." There is much evidence to indicate that the female orgasm is unknown or not experienced (or considered a deviant response not to be divulged). A middle-aged bachelor, who considers himself wise in the ways of the outside world and has a reputation for making love to willing tourists during the summer, described the violent bodily reactions of a girl to his fondling and asked for an explanation; when told the "facts of life," he admitted not knowing that women also could achieve climax, although he was aware that some of them apparently enjoyed lovemaking. Inis Beag men feel that sexual intercourse is debilitating, and they will desist from it the night before they are to perform tasks which will require the expenditure of great energy. Women are approached sexually neither during menstruation nor for at least six months after childbirth, for they are considered "dangerous" to the male at these times. Returned Yanks have been denounced from the pulpit for describing American sexual mores to local youths, and such "pornographic" magazines as *Time* and *Life*, mailed home by relatives from abroad, have aroused curates to spirited sermon and instruction.

Male masturbation seems to be common in Inis Beag (sometimes called the major "escape valve" for frustration in Ireland), but premarital coitus is unknown and marital copulation is limited as to foreplay and the manner of consummation. Elders proudly insist that premarital sexual activities of any sort do not occur in the island, but male youths admit to it in rumor. The claims of young men focus on "petting" with tourists and a few local girls, whom the bolder of them kiss and handle outside of their clothing. Inis Beag girls, it is held by their lovers, do not confess these sins because they fail to experience pleasure from the contact; the male perpetrators also shun the confessional because of their fear of the curate. Absolute privacy at night is sought by married couples when they copulate, and foreplay is limited to kissing and rough fondling of the lower body of the woman, especially her buttocks. Sexual activity invariably is initiated by the husband, and the wife is usually totally passive. Only the male superior position is employed, and intercourse takes place with underclothes not fully removed; orgasm for the man is achieved quickly, after which he falls asleep almost immediately. Whenever I talked with males of sexual practices other than those just described, my remarks were met with disbelief, or I was accused of "codding" my listeners.

Many kinds of behavior disassociated from sex in other societies, such as nudity and physiological evacuation, are considered sexual in Inis Beag. We have noted elsewhere the fear of nudity—which precludes washing the body and bathing in the sea—and the secrecy surrounding the acts of urination and defecation and the use of human manure as fertilizer and cow dung as fuel. The sexual symbolism of nudity not only has resulted in the drowning of seamen who might have saved themselves had they been able to swim, but in the death of men who were unwilling to face the nurse when ill, because it might mean baring their bodies to her, and thus were beyond help when finally treated. An island nurse confided to me that she was physically assaulted by the mother of a young man for diagnosing his illness in the mother's absence and bathing his chest as the woman entered his bedroom. Even the nudity of household pets can arouse anxiety, especially when they are sexually aroused during time of heat. In some cottages, dogs are whipped for licking their genitals and soon learn to indulge in this behavior outside when unobserved.

Hypochondria and depression in Inis Beag are inextricably linked, in that the former composes part of the syndrome of the latter; and just as sexual puritanism is undergirded by masochism, so are these two traits. Little more need be said about the causes of depression among the folk, other than to bring together factors which have been discussed earlier: the extent to which their lives are circumscribed by the will of the priest and other figures of authority; their poverty and the never ending toil needed to maintain present subsistence standards; the spying and malicious gossiping of their fellows and the ubiquity of jealousy and envy; the isolation of the island, particularly during winter months; numbing boredom and the dearth of social activities; for women, the lack of freedom and of attention and affection from their spouses, as well as the necessity of enduring sexual relations; and, as stated above, hypochondria. Much has been written about isolation and its depressive effects on the islanders, and the folk themselves constantly complain of being shut off from the world and prey to wind, rain, fog, and raging sea. But isolation need not lead inevitably to depression, for my wife and I conducted research in another island of Ireland—far distant from and even more inaccessible than Inis Beag—where the inhabitants do not feel isolated and are not depressed.

I have expanded the clinical usage of the term hypochondria to include fears of the spirit as well as fears of the body, for ill health can as often be induced by supernatural forces, and death—whether by disease, injury, or aging—is the ultimate fear with its threat of eternal damnation. Colds, influenza, dyspepsia, migraine headaches, teeth decay, the crippling effects of joint and muscle ailments, hypermetrophy, and mental illness are paramount among health concerns. "Flu" epidemics are frequent in the island and are a chief cause of death among people who have become weakened by old age. As the folk advance in years, they come to spend more time in bed and by the turf fire and venture out less during the winter and when it rains. Drafts are avoided whenever possible, and clothes dampened by seas which wash the canoes or by rain are changed for dry ones at the first opportunity. Colds, flu, indigestion, and headaches more than any other afflictions send the islanders to the nurse for drugs and to their own folk remedies for relief. Dyspepsia is known as "wind" and is thought to result from diet, but the nurses say that most cases of indigestion are the result of tension—"nervous stomach." Nine cases of migraine were reported in Inis Beag during 1959, but many other islanders, most of whom are women, suffer from "nervous headache" which can approach migraine in intensity of pain. Neither my wife nor I were ill during the winter of 1959 and 1960, even though we were abroad in all sorts of inclement weather against the advice of our neighbors; when we began picking wild garlic to season our food, it was reasoned that the condiment afforded us protection against the flu, which reached almost epidemic proportions that year, and as a result this folk medicine was used more widely and consistently than usual.

Nativists and primitivists praise the health and hardiness of the folk and boast of the absence of rheumatism and allied infirmities among them and the sharpness of their sight. But, just as most adults past 30 years of age suffer from decay and loss of teeth, they also suffer from muscle and joint ailments, caused by the "damp and cold," and from far-sightedness. It is not known how many folk wear glasses in the privacy of their homes, but only two persons, both men, wear them publicly—and self-consciously when they do. Most glasses are not prescription made but are purchased in mainland shops after many pairs displayed on the counters have been tested, and often a single pair will serve the needs of all the elders of a household. The islanders among themselves constantly complain of these and other ailments, although some will praise the health and hardiness of the local population in the presence of strangers, to conform to the nativistic and primitivistic stereotype. Probably the most robust of the two dozen islanders past the age of 70 years believes that he will live to be 100 years old, because he continues to be active physically and doesn't "worry about the health;" he accuses his fellows of "worrying themselves into the grave" over matters of body and soul.

The etiology of mental illness as conceived by the islanders is varied and embraces both natural and spiritual realms. "Insanity" stigmatizes the victim and his family, often for many generations, no matter what its cause, and as many psychotics are treated at home—hidden from the probing eyes of strangers—as are incarcerated in the mental institution serving the region of which Inis Beag is a part. Statistics on mental disorders are hard to come by because of the opprobrium attached to insanity, but at least eight of the folk were institutionalized for various periods between 1940 and 1965. Only one of these is a woman and none were violent prior to admission. Inheritance, inbreeding, and the menopause are the natural causes most widely accepted by the islanders, but some claim that heavy blows to the head, acute alcoholism, and even prolonged emotional tension—or "nerves"—can induce insanity. In explaining why a former Inis Beag curate was committed to a mental institution, an old man revealed what is probably the most significant cause of mental illness in Ireland when he said that the constant association of the priest with a pretty housekeeper "drove him mad from frustration;" he advocated that only elderly, plain-appearing women (who will not "gab" everything that they know to "our man") be hired for the task.

Supernatural forces are believed capable of causing not only mental illness, but most other maladies and injuries as well. Pagan dispensers of ill health are vengeful or capricious fairies, ghosts, and witches of the evil eye, while Catholicism provides an unpredictable Devil, a deity who punishes sinful thoughts and deeds in this world as well as in the next, and priests who in Inis Beag often have interpreted the boundaries of sin according to Irish and personal criteria. In the case of certain folk stricken with mental disorders, I have heard specific causes put forth to account for their condition: parents who are second cousins, the evil eye of a neighbor, punishment by God for a particular misdeed, and a priest's curse. A man who mistreated his aged bachelor uncle before his recent death now is haunted with the specter of being struck down from the grave with sickness, injury, or madness by the shade of the uncle seeking revenge. His despair and erratic behavior arouse little sympathy from his fellows, who await the day of reckoning. The stigma of mental illness arises from its designation as inheritable or a sign of the deity's displeasure, both of which may doom those of generations to come. There is a strong suspicion among the folk that other maladies which are deforming or leave physical aftereffects once cured can be transmitted through inheritance. In this category are two mongoloids, one dwarf, one epileptic, one person with goiter, one with a cleft palate, and one who has recovered from poliomyelitis. These disabilities also can stigmatize a family.

Probably the most infamous custom associated with the Irish is their excessive intake of intoxicating drink, and certainly Inis Beag islanders are no exception to the stereotype. Men drink far more than women, but even though the latter widely condemn the practice many are known to send their children to the pubs to procure stout and brandy (ostensibly a general purpose medicine in this case) in disguised containers to be consumed at home. The drinking of the men takes place, for the most part, in the pubs and at parties, and seldom is it indulged in to the extent that the imbibers become physically incapacitated. There were no cases of alcoholism in Inis Beag during 1959, according to the nurse. Although drinking obviously is done to combat depression and boredom, dissolve feelings of shyness and inferiority, alleviate the sense of sin and guilt, and overcome secretiveness which limits extroversion, the folk defend the practice by claiming that it makes them more articulate and convivial and thus better able to sing, dance, converse with one another, and tell stories. The often used phrases "to give us courage" and "great gas" connote just these benefits. In Ireland today, there are nearly half-a-million members of the Pioneer Total Abstinence Society—founded in that country 125 years ago—who have "taken the pledge" not to drink spirits in any form; they wear a small badge shaped like a shield which bears the emblem of the Sacred Heart. Twelve "Pioneers" in Inis Beag have taken a lifetime pledge and about 30 others a two year pledge not to imbibe. Most of these persons are old men, women, and boys. Young and middle–aged men who are members of the society are the objects of a good deal of indirect ridicule and direct jesting.

Folklore

As a result of acculturation, the Inis Beag esthetic tradition today is not nearly so rich as it was two generations ago, nor has it ever been as rich as those found in many other peasant areas of Ireland. The principal esthetic forms are folklore, music, and dance; lacking are the graphic and plastic arts, and of the crafts already considered only the knitting of ganzies, the crocheting of shawls, and *crios* making transcend sheer utility in their manufacture, according to the evaluation of island artisans. Myths, legends, folktales, and anecdotes among prose narratives, and song texts and proverbs, are the predominant genres of oral literature. There is no drama, while poetry, riddles, and jokes seldom are recited.

"Along the western shores of Ireland and Scotland . . . is preserved the oldest vernacular literature in Europe, north and west of the Alps. Along this tattered cultural frontier . . . [are] the last remnants of the most venerable body of orally preserved tradition in western Europe" (Delargy 1957:178). The Inis Beag folk share this body of folklore, and storytelling always has loomed large in the lives of the people. However, it had disappeared formally from the island by the time that my wife and I came, and we were never able to attend a traditional storytelling session, but had to reconstruct its institutionalized characteristics by plumbing the memory of one of the two aged narrators still alive. There are two types of Irish storytellers: the *scéalaí*, who recounts myths and legends of the mythological, Ulster, Fenian, and historical cycles, as well as ancient folktales; and the *seanchaí*, "who makes a specialty of local tales, family-sagas, or genealogies, social-historical tradition, and the like, and can recount many tales of a short realistic type about fairies, ghosts, and other supernatural beings (Delargy 1945:6). In Inis Beag, the former type of storyteller was always male and the latter usually male but sometimes female. Also, the former occupied a higher prestige position than the latter, but there was not the clear-cut distinction between genres appropriate to each type of narrator as elsewhere in Ireland; the *seanchaí* sometimes related the exploits of Finn and the *scéalaí* the pranks of the red man. The two surviving storytellers in 1960 were both old men, but the *seanchaí* died in 1963 and the *scéalaí* two years later. Both had been prolific contributors to Irish Folklore Commission collectors and Continental folklorists.

All of the above kinds of folklore expression, with the exception of folktales, were regarded as true by island folk in the past. The myths either coexisted or were reinterpreted with Biblical stories, and the legends were synchronized with events of ancient world history dating from just before the Flood to the eighth century. The Inis Beag *scéalaí* sometimes was derided by school children for still believing his narratives to be true, as was the *seanchaí* for claiming that the supernatural happenings described in his tales actually were experienced by islanders in the past century. Both narrators for many years had been visited only by folklorists and tourists wishing to hear them relate their repertoires of stories, for the only form of storytelling which has been perpetuated is the occasional gathering of men in a home or pub to exchange anecdotes, mostly related to fishing. I was told that in his prime the *scéalaí* could have recited narratives nightly for "at least a month" without ever repeating a story, had he ever been called on to do so. That the memory of the esteemed narrator is prodigious is revealed in the complete collection of all the material recorded from a single *scéalaí* of Co. Kerry, reported by Delargy, which included 396 pages of text: 186 tales, a few songs and song fragments, and various smaller items of prose and verse. These had been obtained from 27 different sources by the narrator, all of whom save one were neighbors (Delargy 1945:11).

Most liked by the folk were the prose narratives related by the *scéalaí* and tales of recent and contemporary historical events in the region, stories of the supernatural in Inis Beag, and personal experiences told by the *seanchaí*. Few of the stories dealt with historical occurrences in Ireland between the coming of Christianity and the beginning of the nineteenth century, and none of them concerned personages or happenings associated with the church. At my request, the *seanchaí* read three books of Irish folklore that I had brought with me—J. J. Campbell's *Legends of Ireland*, Jeremiah Curtin's *Irish Folk-Tales*, and Eileen O'Faolain's *Irish Sagas and Folk-Tales*—and declared that he had heard all of the stories therein as a youth from his father and other island storytellers. However, the versions in the books often were "incorrect," he claimed, and he delighted in "correcting" them; of course, there are many variants of each tale (as many as 527—Aarne-Thompson type 300 in the archives of the Irish Folklore Commission), and he regarded the Inis Beag stories as the legitimate variants. Most of the local and Irish tales share types (plots) and motifs (incidents, characters, and objects) with those of European and other societies brought about by millennia of diffusion, but the Irish have refashioned these elements in their own corpus according to their culture and personality dispositions.

I will not discuss the various prose narratives told by the *scéalaí* of Inis Beag; the greater number of them can be obtained from Campbell or O'Faolain or Sean O'Sullivan's recent *Folktales of Ireland*. But a further word must be said of the tales recited by the *seanchaí*. Popular among local legends are those dealing with such topics as the famine, evictions and other excesses of past landlords, visits to the island by the Black and Tans seeking political refugees, shipwrecks, and tragedies at sea among fishermen. Stories of the supernatural center around the actions of fairies, the pookah and banshee, those with the evil eye, phantom ships, mermaids and sea demons, and material objects possessing human attributes and volitions. These local legends sometimes qualify as anecdotes, and it is humorous anecdotes which the folk refer to as jokes. Outsiders—such as returned Yanks— are responsible for introducing true jokes, but often these are not told and soon are forgotten, especially if they are "dirty jokes." There is no indigenous dirty joking tradition because of sexual puritanism. I have heard men use various verbal devices—innuendos, puns, and asides—that they believed bear sexual connotations; relatively speaking, they are pallid. In the song that I composed, one line of a verse refers to an islander who arose late on the morning of the shipwreck after "dreaming perhaps of a beautiful mate;" this is regarded as a highly suggestive phrase, and I have seen it redden cheeks and lower glances in a pub.

Storytelling in the past took place mostly between the last week of October and early January, when inclement weather forced a slackening of the fishing regime, and the Christmas season kept people in and near their homes. Nowadays, card playing almost nightly during November and part of December by many of the men has become a substitute activity, which excludes the participation of women and children who once composed a part of the audience addressed by the storyteller. At any one time during this period, several groups met to hear Inis Beag narrators; a *scéalaí* or *seanchaí* might be visited by a group and serve as host, or he might be invited into or visit on his own another household, and word of his presence would quickly draw an audience. The session lasted from eight or nine o'clock until midnight, and a tale might be so long that its telling occupied an entire evening, or even two or three consecutive nights. After completing a brief narrative, the storyteller might call on a colleague in the audience to recite a sequel, or the hearers might request that he continue or urge another to contribute a tale.

The average sized audience was composed of a dozen persons, although as many as 20 might attend a session. Small children seldom were allowed in the room unless they were members of the family of the host, nor were women of another household; the children were admonished to sit quietly and not to talk or whisper, and the women knitted or crocheted while listening. Seated in a semi-circle around the hearth, the hearers were faced by the narrator who was seated on the right side of the fireplace, and the wife of the host on the left. Refreshments never were served, but a clay pipe was passed around among the men and very old women. The host furnished pipe and tobacco, and the pipe was passed back to him by each person in turn after being puffed on for several minutes. Only if the story was a long one was the pipe proffered by the host to the narrator from time to time.

Most storytellers were men past the age of 60 years, but some were between 40 and 60 and a few even younger. An old narrator of reputation often called on a young man to recite in order to give him practice, if he felt that the neophyte had the makings of a *scéalaí* or *seanchaí*. When the young storyteller performed publicly, he had to be certain of himself, for if he paused too often or too long or left out portions of the tale, he was ridiculed by the islanders and not called on again. Stories were repeated frequently and enjoyed equally each time by the listeners if told well; sometimes the audience requested a favorite tale, and particular narrators came to be associated with certain stories and always were asked to relate them.

Myths, legends, and folktales told by the *scéalaí* and the long established stories of the *seanchaí* never were embellished but told as accurately as possible. If a narrator attempted to alter such a tale, members of the audience would interrupt and correct him. Stories newly acquired by the folk were modified initially by those who introduced them and by subsequent narrators for a spell, but gradually they became standardized until the point was reached when no one telling them could effect further alterations. The fact that storytellers believed their tales added to the joy of hearing them, for the narrators became deeply involved emotionally in the events that they were describing, and their enthusiasm infected their listeners.

The following were the qualities possessed by a skilled storyteller: he told tales often and derived great pleasure from doing so; he had a musical voice when speaking in either Gaelic or English; he spoke slowly and used few bodily movements; he knew when to pause for effect, especially after a notable incident in the story, which allowed the hearers to picture it in their minds and savor it; his pauses seldom exceeded ten seconds, and he did not cough or interject "bedad," "begob," or "musha" while pausing (an indication that he was trying to recall the next portion of the tale); he looked at each member of the audience in turn, and often stared down at the floor or into the fire for a time; and, he smiled but did not laugh after relating an episode which aroused merriment among his listeners.

When a storyteller was called on, he thought for a spell, head in hands, instead of immediately launching into his tale, even though he probably had made a choice long before. He did not need the urging of the audience or the "courage" afforded by whiskey or stout—which singers and dancers do today—in order to perform. Once started, he never rose from the hob in the hearth, and if he gestured too much in attempting to enact the tale he was laughed at. Interruptions other than corrections were not countenanced; no words of encouragement or praise were uttered as in singing and dancing; and no one dared sleep during a session. The late *scéalaí* carried a short sally rod which he used to prod listeners who appeared to be weary. It is alleged that he once tried to gouge the eyes of a nodding youth with his forked fingers, an incident which often is alluded to when his past performances are recollected.

Contrary to the opinion of nativists, storytellers of the past in Inis Beag were as proficient in English as in Irish, and tales were told in both tongues with equal ease and audience appreciation. The same cannot be said of proverbs, however, for the folk seldom employ them in their English speech. Proverbs figure prominently in the vernacular and are brief and pithy; their adroit use is a mark of erudition and elegance of speech, and they are used in ordinary conversation to add color and give point: to guide, to encourage, to praise, to admonish, to reprove, and to implement the art of "indirection" so dear to the Irish. Many are subtle and cannot be understood unless the history and culture of Inis Beag and Ireland are known to the listener. Such a one is, "Come raise the bag on me." This proverb derives from the days of the famine, when maize (corn) was distributed to the poor and hungry; an old woman on the mainland nearby with eight mouths to feed was given a one pound sack, and she asked an official to help her with the "great load." Now it is employed whenever someone receives less than he anticipated. Both tales and proverbs serve enculturative ends by providing models of proper behavior to infants and children. Riddles, told only by the very young, also function in this manner—to sharpen the wits.

Music, Song, and Dance

Many times I have heard it said on the mainland that the folk of Inis Beag were in the past, and still are, "poor" musicians, singers, and dancers. It is claimed that once there were competent "fiddlers," pipers, tin whistle and flute players, and accordion, concertina, and melodeon players in the island, but during the months that my wife and I lived there, our portable phonograph and two dozen records —along with the accordions of several inexpert musicians, mostly young men trying to master the instrument—provided most of the music for dancing. Music also is produced by lilting, which is known as "mouth music" or "*pus* music" (*pus* being a Gaelic word for mouth). I have witnessed only one man lilt to accompany step dancing, and he for never more than three minutes without pause because of his advanced age; at 73 years, he can lilt while dancing a brief jig himself.

The violin is played holding its base in the crook of the elbow, while the forearm is supported on the thigh of the seated musician. The sole fiddler in 1960 was the *seanchaí*, and he could step dance, sing, and recite poetry as well with a high order of excellence for a man of 72 years. Much more difficult to play than its mouth blown counterpart of Scottish fame, the Irish Uilleann bagpipe is played while seated, and its windbag inflated by a bellow manipulated by movements of the upper arm. Since its drone pipes do not dominate the chanter, or melody pipe, the music produced with this bagpipe is more tuneful than that of the Highland instrument: as one islander put it, "The Scottish pipes make you want to charge into battle, while ours make you want to leap up and dance." Today, the only pipe music heard in Inis Beag is played during the summer, when occasionally a mainland piper is hired to furnish music to dance to for children attending summer language school. Tin whistle players usually perform on the flute also, since the former instrument is a smaller, vertically played cousin of the latter, somewhat resembling the recorder. It is extremely common on the mainland, but no longer played in Inis Beag except infrequently by visitors. Although the accordion and related wind instruments have achieved a new popularity owing to the vogue of the "*céilí* band," in which they assume a commanding position, they were played widely in the island during the last century after being introduced by lighthouse and coast guard personnel. Only four tunes are played by Inis Beag accordionists to accompany dancing.

Instrumentalists, lilters, and singers traditionally performed individually; music was played by a fiddler or flutist and sung by a lilter only to serve solo and figure dancers, and a singer never was joined by others in chorus or accompanied by an instrument. But now the dancers, young and old alike, choose to dance to the lively jigs and reels of the *céilí* band, which plays modern Irish "country dance music." My wife and I discovered that the folk preferred our *céilí* band records for dancing, and were reticent about performing to the music of our many records of fiddling, piping, and flute and tin whistle playing of exceptional quality. On several occasions, we played jazz and classical recordings to groups assembled in our home, to which the islanders listened politely but indifferently. Our *céilí* band records seemed to be quite as acceptable as an accordion at dances and in the pub, and I frequently shared equally with an instrumentalist the time spent in furnishing music for a night long party.

Of the Irish song tradition, Donal O'Sullivan writes: "There is, indeed, a consensus of informed opinion as to its exceeding beauty. . . . In sheer abundance, also, it is probably not surpassed by that of any nation of comparable area and population: for this small and thinly inhabited island has yielded . . . many thousands of melodies of unusual diversity—all of them the anonymous product of the people . . ." (O'Sullivan 1961:5). The Inis Beag folk, as in the case of their music, share but a small portion of this vast body of song. Only a few songs sung publicly by less than a dozen islanders are in Irish, and these are predominantly local compositions. Most of the songs have texts in English and are common to the mainland as well, and of these but a handful are true folk songs—"anonymous product of the people"—rather than broadsides (printed, sold, and memorized) of the eighteenth and nineteenth centuries. Tunes and songs, just as tale types and motifs, of the Irish often are shared with British and Continental neighbors, and it is hard to know their points of origin and paths of diffusion. Some islanders believe that a few of their songs—such as "The Pretty Maid Milking Her Cow"— were obtained by overhearing the fairies at play. Only one composer is active in the vicinity of Inis Beag at the present time; he is a young man from Inis Thiar who excels at composing songs in Irish based on recent events of importance in and near the two islands. A song of his, which describes the incidents arising out of the grounding of the steamer on a sand bar off Inis Thiar several years ago, is one of the most sung ballads in the region.

Singing is a popular pastime in Inis Beag, particularly among men in the pubs, and several islanders of both sexes have outstanding voices by Irish standards. I tape recorded only 38 songs (13 in Gaelic) and found their major themes to be sentimental, patriotic, and humorous—stressing death, unrequited love, emigration and the parting of relatives and friends, conflict in various forms with the English, and lives of the political "martyrs." Love songs, lullabies, humorous songs, religious songs, laments, drinking songs, and songs of occupation (such as ploughing, milking, and spinning) are the major indigenous Irish folk song categories (O'Sullivan 1961:39), but some are absent and others are under-represented in Inis Beag. Also absent are carols, as well as boat songs like those of the Gaelic speaking Scottish fishermen. Only a few tunes accommodate the songs sung in the island, and the text is far more important to listeners than the ability of a singer to carry the melody. Much admired is the person who can sing a long ballad without pausing or making a mistake, and each episode of the song is listened to attentively, while an occasional, "God be with you.", "Good man.", or "That's it." from the audience urges the singer on or rewards his efforts.

The records of songs that my wife and I brought to Inis Beag with us feature performers who sing in both Gaelic and English, and the latter were favored by the islanders. Contrary to our expectations, they disliked our Gael Linn records from Dublin, because they could not understand the Irish of the singers; nor did they care for a commercial record cut in a nearby island, for the ethnocentric reason that the singers there are thought to be inferior to their own. We soon had to learn folk songs, as we often were "called out" to sing, but our American songs although admired as to melody, did not arouse the interest of our listeners as to text. "The Cowboy's Lament," once learned, came to be "my song" and was always requested at parties; it is now sung by others in my absence, but never when I am in the island. Just as this song appeals to the masochism of the folk, my wife's singing of "The Lavender Cowboy"—"who had only two hairs on his chest"—in a pub aroused their sexual puritanism, and was never sung again after its introduction because of the embarrassed response of the men. Since we ordered many Irish folksong books in order to learn texts, island singers borrowed them to commit to memory additional texts themselves, and they also requested that we give them texts of "cowboy songs" taken from records.

My ballad was prompted by the absence of an indigenous composer, some impromptu rhyming that I had done in the pubs, an eye witness account of the rescue (written by my wife but dictated by me, according to local opinion) which appeared in a Dublin newspaper, and was urged on me by my respondents. I chose the air of the popular broadside song, "Brian O'Linn," and copied the lyric style of its composer, and based as many verses as possible on the more prevalent rumors which arose in the months following the shipwreck. Copying the folklore idiom as accurately as I could, I also employed many Irish terms—especially place-names—and eschewed Yank expressions while incorporating local ones at every opportunity. In time, island balladiers came to substitute words and phrases, and even stanzas, as they molded the song more closely to their tongue and milieu. Some lines came to be used as proverbs and others to stimulate a variety of conversational responses.

Little is known of the history of Irish dancing. The earliest references to round and long dances are from the sixteenth century, and they appear to be older than the single, or "step," dances. The step and figure dances of today were created by the dancing masters of the eighteenth and nineteenth centuries (O'Keeffe and O'Brien 1912:13–27). Step dancing preceded figure dancing in Inis Beag, although there is a difference of opinion among elders as to whether or not the coast guard families introduced figure dancing a hundred years ago. Young adults no longer step dance, although since 1960 children have been stimulated to learn the skill through instruction in the school and by watching and participating in the dances of the students attending summer language school; so this may rejuvenate the moribund tradition. However, several men past the age of 40 years still are able to perform jigs, reels, hornpipes, and hop-jigs with dexterity, "when the humor is on them," and are called out at parties and in the pubs; a few women will step dance in their homes or at small social gatherings.

There is considerable evidence to suggest that the rigid body and arms of the step dancer are an early nineteenth century product of Jansenist doctrine in the church, which attempted to desexualize dancing. Most of the movement is below the hips of the dancer, and it is the feet of the performer which are watched intently by the audience, at least openly. Inis Beag men move their upper bodies and arms more than is customary on the mainland, and they are not as graceful as other Irish dancers.

Figure dancing is called "set" dancing in Ireland, and there are many such dances, each of which combines a number of simple and complex figures performed by the couples. There is only one set in Inis Beag; it bears no name and is danced by one or more groups of four couples each. The many figures of the dance are simple, and it takes about 20 minutes to complete. I have heard young dancers complain at the end of a night of the tediousness of the single set, and some of them are learning other Irish figures at language school dances—"The Walls of Limerick" and "The Bridge of Athlone," among others. The most enjoyed movement of the local set is the one at the end in which the man holds his partner closely and twirls her almost violently, sometimes for longer than is prescribed so that the musician must pause or alter his rhythm. With bodily contact between partners otherwise so limited, perhaps this figure allows the expression of repressed sexuality.

Parties

It is appropriate to describe the Inis Beag party and a festive night at the pub in this chapter, because they are esthetic as well as social events, in which are combined storytelling, music, song, and dance. Parties are very much the same, whether held in the winter or the summer or to welcome home a long departed emigrant or to "drag home" a new bride. Only two rooms of the house are utilized —the kitchen and "the room" adjoining it—and benches are placed along the walls to supplement the chairs and bed on which guests will sit. The barrel or two of stout to be served is placed in the back hall off the kitchen, if there is such a hall, or in a back corner of the kitchen, and one man is assigned the task of dispensing the drink and remaining at his post throughout the night. Another man acts as "pourer" and fills a bucket from which he pours the stout into several mugs and glasses which are circulated from man to man. A bottle of whiskey is opened and proffered only to the old men, who often sit in a group beside the fireplace and exchange anecdotes and tales. On a table in "the room" are placed bottles of wine and soft drinks to accommodate the women and non-drinkers among the men before and after refreshments are served. Sometimes an elderly woman will drink surreptitiously of the whiskey or stout, and it is customary for the musicians and those who sing and step dance the most to be awarded extra amounts of stout. Women tend to drink very little at parties, in part because of the embarrassment caused them by visiting the outside toilet with men looking on.

The party commences with several sets danced in quick succession. There is room for only one dance group initially because of the small size of the kitchen and the large number of guests filling the house. It is difficult to move about the two rooms with the press of bodies, and the crowd within is matched by the cluster of men around the front door awaiting their turn to dance. Unmarried women tend to sit and stand on one side of the kitchen and men on the other, while married people congregate in the other room. Children in their best dress sit quietly together and watch the festivities tirelessly until the guests depart. Crowding at the party necessitates that men and women will be pressed together both as dancers and viewers, and that persons will sit on one anothers' laps, including women on the laps of men occasionally. The islanders strain to display indifference, as they do in watching a full-bodied woman step dance, at least until the intake of alcohol causes a few to betray their emotions.

Usually two or even three accordionists (and the visiting anthropologist with his phonograph) are invited to attend, and they spell one another. After an hour or so of dancing, singers and step dancers perform between the sets while stout is poured; they may be called out by the urging of the guests, or by the host or one of his choosing who acts as a master of ceremonies and directs all of the activities of the party. Stout may be distributed during the sets, but most hosts prefer that it be done during pauses, so that less is spilled by the dancing and milling crowd. The pourer with his bucket follows the movement of the mugs and glasses as they are passed about, and each man on having his container filled drains it quickly and surrenders it to another nearby. Most of the young men visit the pubs before the party and may do so again once or twice before the pubs close.

Midway during the night, the table of "the room" is set, and refreshments are served to all of the guests in shifts. First the women are served, then the children, followed by the young men who do not drink stout, and finally the other men. Both in viewing the proceedings from benches and in eating, the children are separated as to sex. The menu resembles that of the usual Inis Beag meal and includes tea, bread spread with butter and jam, cakes, and sometimes hard candy. Between the many sittings, the dishes and utensils are washed in a bucket and the table reset. Dancing continues in the kitchen during this period, and after everyone is served the table is moved to a corner and a second set is formed. The remainder of the night is spent in dancing, but the pauses which punctuate the sets become longer and the songs and step dances by guests more frequent as dawn approaches.

My wife and I sponsored a Christmas party in 1959 in the home of an islander and invited the entire population of Inis Beag. Two hours after midnight, when I was absent briefly escorting an old man to his cottage, a fight broke out between two family factions which sent all of the guests scurrying home. The following day, everyone whom we met commiserated with us "for the shame of it," and we were told of many other parties in the past which had ended in the same manner, so that we would not think our affair a failure. In recent years, "rowdyism" on the part of youths who have "taken too much" has increased at parties, so that many islanders will not give them for fear of possible damage to houses and outbuildings. The reason why one man is assigned to the barrel of stout and a "firm" master of ceremonies is favored is to curb drunkenness and factional fighting. Small parties are coming to replace the large ones of the past, with invitations tendered secretly and at the last moment to avoid attracting "hooligans." The format, however, has remained the same.

Pubs

Both pubs in Inis Beag do a thriving business. There are some folk who purchase all of their provisions, drinks, and tobacco in only one of the pubs, others who buy most of them in one but occasionally do business in the second, and still others who scrupulously balance their buying between the two. The first group is composed of near kin of the publicans, and the second of those who are economically beholden to the king and utilize his pub mostly, or who dislike him and give the lion's share of their business to the other. This pattern is broken only when one of the pubs is out of a commodity which the other has in stock, one of them is closed for whatever reason, a "big night" is taking place at one of them, or a dispute interferes. During the day, provisions are purchased in the shop—by children, women, and sometimes men; the women and children make their visits as brief as possible, but the men are likely to stay for at least one "pint" of stout and a "smoke." Other visitors in the daytime are chronic drinkers, men who are working nearby and use the pub for a break, and men reciprocating for economic services rendered. The pub is the province of the adult males at night, and the only women who enter are the teachers, visiting emigrants, and tourists. Seldom is step dancing done unless outsiders are present, and when women are in the audience they will be called out to form a set or to dance solo or be paired with an islander. Some nights only two or three of the folk will put in an appearance at the pub, but on other nights as many as 20 persons will crowd into the narrow room, while others in the hallway and outside wait to take their turn inside. Another half-dozen men may sit in the snug drinking and talking together privately.

Men come to the pub after dark usually in groups of two, three, or four. Reciprocity dictates the drinking procedure, with each man in a group taking his turn at "standing a round" for as long as the evening lasts. Men who do not like to drink much or have little money will come to the pub singly or with another in like circumstances, so that they will not become victims of the custom of reciprocation. My first experience with this custom—in 1958 in a neighboring island— almost ended in tragedy for me, as I was with six men who insisted on drinking "glasses" of whiskey; only my deep commitment to research and a heavy meal a short time before prevented a "third round knockout." The first hour after the men arrive in the pub is a quiet one, as they sit in silence or whisper to one another while drinking pints in rapid succession. As their shyness gradually is overcome by alcohol, they become more talkative and speak in louder tones to a wider circle of their fellows. At least two hours must pass before individuals have "courage" enough to tell stories to all assembled or to sing. The best singers will be called out with shouts of encouragement from the others, and some men need as many as five minutes of urging before they will perform. In the case of the man who is particularly reticent about singing, those sitting on either side of him will grasp his hands with one of theirs and swing his arms backward and forward until he commences to sing in the suggested rhythm of the arm movements. Sometimes this continues throughout the song, and later in the evening it is done with other singers as the sense of male "camaraderie" grows apace.

Seldom does fighting break out in the pub, for the publican will not serve drinks to those whom he feels have taken too much, and he will order everyone out if there is a threat of violence. Visiting women invariably are treated politely no matter how boisterous the men become. On a nearby island, my wife and I saw a Yank brutally beaten and thrown out of a pub by several men when he spoke "disrespectfully" in Gaelic before us and another visiting women. An elderly widower of Inis Beag was much criticized when after dancing with my wife in a pub he brushed his check against hers briefly in his exuberance; she thought nothing of it, but many of the folk apologized to her for his action, and our relationship with the man thereafter was strained. Visitors must be careful about how they participate in the drinking pattern of the pub. If they drink by themselves or only with outsiders and never buy rounds for the islanders present, they are despised secretly; but if they stand rounds often with the obvious end in view of earning acceptance, they are considered "fools." The several folk who will take advantage of a stranger who is generous with rounds in the pub are subjected to severe censure. Each year, my wife and I donate a barrel of stout to a pub on St. Partick's Day to be drunk by islanders who come that night—to commemorate the shipwreck and rescue (whose anniversary is nine days before); a verse of my ballad refers to certain folk who will not accept drinks unless they can reciprocate—"People will say the free stout brought me in."

┌─────────┐
│   5   │
└─────────┘

The Future of the Island

Emigration

MANY ELDERS IN INIS BEAG fear that the island and its neighbors will go the way of the Blasket Islands of Co. Kerry, whose remaining inhabitants were removed by the government because their support had become an economic liability. With only slight fluctuations, the population of Inis Beag has been diminishing since it reached its zenith of 532 persons in 1861. Below are population figures since 1821—when the first census was compiled—until the present time:

1821	421
1841	456
1861	532
1881	497
1901	483
1926	409
1936	445
1946	447
1956	376
1960	350

The upsurge in population after 1926 reflects the depression in the United States and the Second World War, when emigrants returned home to escape unemployment and conscription, while the downsurge after 1946 reflects the shift of emigration from America to England. Frequently discussed by elders is the steady increase in emigration during the past 15 years, the decreasing age of emigrants, and the presence within the past decade—for the first time in three centuries—of aged parents all of whose children have emigrated, and of land which is idle or rented out by emigrants who probably never will return to Inis Beag. Jokes concerning the building of a hotel by the Germans or a missile site by the Americans in the island to stimulate the economy, as well as serious suggestions that the

124

government increase its services and subsidies even more, reveal the underlying tension within those who are most strongly committed to the local tradition and wish its perpetuation.

The index of my field notes contains more references to emigration than to any other category, for seldom in an interview, whether guided or open-ended, did the topic fail to come up, no matter what was the initial subject under consideration. Of the more than 30 causes of the phenomenon yielded by my analysis, all are known to the folk, and they are ever eager to express opinions as to the relative weights which should be attached to those that they deem significant. My wife and I usually were solicited for our opinions as well whenever the topic was addressed. I will deal below with only the major causes of emigration from Inis Beag, and will consider first those which are internal—the "push" factors—and then those which are external—the "pull" factors. The islanders emphasize external causes in their own deliberations, but those who are not apologists for the *status quo*, or who are genuinely bewildered by the exodus of young people in recent years, are able to identify the internal ones also, but are less willing to assign them sufficient weight. Emigration is the topic about which my wife and I could be most objective and outspoken concerning the role of the church and obtain the most agreement and arouse the least resentment among our respondents.

Paramount among the push factors are the previously considered system of inheritance and the causes underlying the prevalence of celibacy, late marriage, and personality depression. The fact that only one son in a family can inherit land, which forces his brothers to emigrate, is the internal factor most stressed in the literature pertaining to Inis Beag, but least stressed by the folk. The reason for this is that until recently it was rather common for siblings without land to remain on the island, thanks to the benevolence of their brothers and the government and their ability to support themselves by craft work, keeping tourists, fishing, managing shops, and obtaining remittances. Of the 71 households in Inis Beag, 28 are headed by male siblings: 20 in which 10 pairs of brothers and their families live, 3 in which 3 pairs of bachelor siblings reside, 3 in which 3 brothers and their families live, and 2 in which 3 siblings reside—two as bachelors in one and the third with his family in the other. It is apparent that other factors, of equal or greater importance, are stimulating emigration.

The push factor given the most weight by the islanders is the unwillingness of men to marry—"The lads are too fussy, and the girls get tired of waiting and go off." But the fact that male "fussiness" is based on such conditions as parents opposing the marriage of their sons for various reasons and bachelors being loath to assume the responsibilities of marriage, especially its sexual responsibilities, seldom is probed. Sometimes it is the girls who are accused of "putting off" potential spouses by being too discriminating, but this accusation becomes untenable when one observes that there is but a single unmarried woman between the ages of 26 and 44 years in Inis Beag (as compared to 18 men), and that the average age at which women emigrate has dropped from 24.5 years during the 1941–1950 decade to 21.1 during the last decade (as compared to 24.9 to 23.8 for men). Some girls admit that they are emigrating because the possibility of their being asked to marry is remote, but far more of them are dissatisfied with the lot of married

women in the island and are attracted by what they consider to be a more reward-
ing life on the mainland and abroad, and so emigrate for these reasons. One of the
most "pitied" girls in the island is a returned emigrant to the United States, who,
despite being 24 years of age and suitable for marriage in every way, is not being
courted, although it is known that she came back to Inis Beag to obtain a husband.

All of the conditions making for personality depression—the intrusion of
priests into secular affairs, hypochondria, malicious gossiping, poverty, boredom,
and isolation—also instigate emigration. My analysis assigns the secular excesses
of the clergy and their implementation of the Jansenist doctrines of the Catholic
Church in Ireland as the primary push factors in emigration and supports the
contention made by Paul Blanshard that, "When all the reasons for a flight from
Ireland have been mentioned, there still remains a suspicion that Irish young
people are leaving their nation largely because it is a poor place in which to be
happy and free. Have the priests created a civilization in which the chief values
of youth and love are subordinate to Catholic discipline?" (Blanshard 1954:154).
What "remains a suspicion" to Blanshard as regards all of Ireland is very much a
reality in Inis Beag.

Other internal factors accounting for emigration which are considered
important by the folk are the deadening of initiative by government services and
subsidies and the institutionalization of emigration itself. While many islanders
believe that the government ought to support even further the local economy in
order to combat emigration, others feel that its present level of benevolence has
had a deleterious effect on their character. Young people observing the indolence
of their elders, according to this opinion, are shamed into seeking a more active
life away from Inis Beag. In my estimation, this is a superficial cause, but the
institutionalization of emigration is a vital factor, more recognized by youth than
by their parents. Just as in the case of late marriage, emigration since famine times
gradually has become an expectation—a "way of life"—and it will stimulate some
folk to leave even though, in the estimation of their fellows, it might be advan-
tageous for them to remain. When a young man says that he has an "itch to go
to England and work for a spell," he usually is being motivated in this manner.

Among the external causes of emigration, the most significant are the
growth of prosperity on the mainland and abroad, the influence of ever increasing
numbers of tourists who visit and returned emigrants who come for short stays
or to retire in Inis Beag, the impact of the mass media of communication, and the
increasing availability of scholarship funds for children to attend secondary schools
on the mainland. The United States has been a land of freedom, opportunity, and
prosperity to the Irish since the early seventeenth century, but particularly during
and after the famine (Approximately 1,000,000 Irish emigrated between 1846
and 1851, and another 1,500,000 perished from hunger, according to Woodham-
Smith 1962:411.). The first record of substantial emigration from Inis Beag is in
1822, and from that time until the Second World War most islanders migrated
to the United States, never to return. However, with the growth of prosperity in
England after 1946, the stream of emigration shifted in that direction. Not only
did jobs become plentiful across the Irish Sea then, but large, viable ethnic communities served by Irish clergy had sprung up in the larger cities. It became possi-

ble to visit Inis Beag frequently, as the cost and distance are slight compared to a journey across the Atlantic.

The many vacationing emigrants who now return to the island at Christmas or Easter or during the summer months often succeed in persuading relatives and acquaintances to return to England with them. Those so persuaded declare that they will return soon with their "fortunes" to settle permanently, but they seldom do once "emancipated." Since the Second World War, several Americans have returned home, and their stories of life in the United States make the youth restive. Tourists who remain for weeks and months in Inis Beag and come to know many islanders also sow the seeds of discontent. A favorite subject of talk in the pubs is the relative advantages to be gained from migrating to particular cities in England and America, and anthropologists as well as returned emigrants are called on as consultants in this matter by youths.

Almost every cottage in Inis Beag has a radio, or "wireless," and although the folk seldom read books, a wide assortment of domestic and foreign magazines and newspapers find their way into most homes. These mass media also are an emancipating force making for restiveness and discontent, because they allow islanders a glimpse behind the "lace curtain" at what appears to be a happier and freer world. Television was introduced into Inis Beag in 1963 at the lighthouse, and a second set was procured for the new "dance hall" when it was completed two years later. Few islanders venture to the lighthouse to view television, but I am told by correspondents that many now visit the hall during the several evening hours when transmission from Telefis Eireann takes place. As a result, television has become an acculturative medium to be reckoned with. Both radio and television programs are censored in Ireland, but even so the morality expressed in them—especially in the sex and violence drenched American ones—presents a striking contrast to locally conceived moral precepts. A hypothetical censor from Inis Beag most certainly would create more discontinuities with his shears in television performances than would his much maligned "secularized" colleagues in Dublin. My wife and I found that viewing television with islanders at the lighthouse on two occasions was a traumatic experience; it gave us a different (and even more disquieting) perspective on programs in the United States and their enculturative effects than can be obtained at home.

Since the Second World War, 28 island youths have pursued secondary education elsewhere in Ireland, either in high schools, called "colleges," or in technical schools, and most have been supported by government scholarships. The usual high school scholarship is for 5 years, and a student must be 14 years of age and qualify by competitive examination to receive one. Only 4 of these 28 students —of which 2 are teachers in the national school—have returned to Inis Beag. One young man watched 2 girls, either of whom he eventually might have married, go off to the mainland for school and said, "Scholarships are killing the island;" what he was referring to, other than his own disappointment, is the fact that 19 of the 28 students who left for advanced education are girls. The reason for the disproportionate number of girls receiving scholarships is that they are far more motivated academically and have better scholastic records than boys. There is, however, a widespread belief in the island that certain families are favored by priests and teachers, whose influence and attention earn for the children of these families the greater share of scholarship funds.

Not only has education abroad been a major pull factor in emigration, but local education as well in the form of a summer language school for mainland children, which was established in 1960 and has convened for two months each year ever since. Over a hundred students—in two shifts of a month apiece— attend the school, where in addition to learning Irish formally and speaking it in the homes where they are lodged, they are instructed in singing, playing musical instruments, and set dancing in the traditional mold. Monies from Gaeltacht Eireann support the director from the mainland and the Inis Beag headmaster who teach, a skilled musician who provides music for dancing and also instructs, and the students. Eight hundred pounds were channeled into the local economy in 1960 by this nativistic endeavor hopefully aimed at propagating Gaelic and halting emigration. The influence of the visiting children, who interact with their island counterparts at home and at outdoor dances each evening, is considerable; the outsiders tend to be critical of conditions in Inis Beag and boast of the superiority in every dimension of life on the mainland. It is questionable whether the school has diminished the push effect of emigration by enlivening the social atmosphere of the island as much as it has increased the pull effect by creating even more discontent among young people. There are those who denounce the language school on the grounds that the visiting children speak more English than Irish in the local homes; that many islanders in their greed for profit do not provide adequately for the students assigned to them; and that some of the mainlanders are openly promiscuous and thus subvert the morality of Inis Beag youths.

Since 1960, priests have become more realistic in their appraisal of the causes of emigration and have taken steps to enliven further the social milieu of the island. They have been responsible for introducing set dancing and tin whistle playing instruction in the national school, for organizing yearly athletic, canoe rowing, and dancing competitions between folk of Inis Beag and Inis Thiar, for building the dance hall to serve various purposes, and for setting up a small lending library of books in the school. The hall was built with a Gaeltacht Eireann grant, the free labor of island men, and money gifts solicited from interested parties all over the world. It resembles its predecessor—the boathouse on the strand built by the coast guard company—in that it functions as dance hall, trade school, storage house, and meeting place; but it is much larger and better constructed and has many more facilities than the latter. The folk view it as a mixed blessing, for they disliked building it without being paid wages, and feel now that it is not available to them enough of the time, and when it is, they are charged by the curate to attend dances and view television. Many believe that church and government should have provided wages to the builders to compensate for farming and other time lost, and that "the key of the hall shouldn't be in the priest's pocket." Since its completion, the building has accommodated most of the activities of the language school.

In contrast to the islanders who are deeply committed to the local culture and fear that Inis Beag will become depopulated within the next generation, there are those who are either indifferent to the rapid increase in emigration since 1946, or welcome it. The island has its bitter critics, even among a few of the oldest generation who regret not having emigrated when they had the opportunity. A noted craftsman, long disillusioned with island existence, is refusing to train any of his sons to carry on the family tradition of generations. English is spoken as much as Irish in the presence of children in some households so as to prepare them for eventual emigration, in spite of the protestations of some priests and neighbors who insist that the alien tongue not be spoken on moral and nativistic grounds. The language revival movement receives much criticism because it results in emigrants being placed at a disadvantage; a frequently heard utterance in Inis Beag, even among those who hesitate to use English before their offspring, is, "What good will Irish do a person?" It is customary now for emigrating youths with inadequate command of English to spend three months to a year in a mainland community—with relatives or at a job—before going on to England or America. On the mainland, they also overcome some of their shyness and feelings of inferiority and become acquainted with Western customs absent from Inis Beag.

Islanders Abroad

My wife and I obtained some emigration statistics for the siblings of all folk now living in Inis Beag. For 289 persons who emigrated between 1891 and 1958, we assembled accurate data on: community settled in abroad, occupation, marriage age, place of origin and religion of spouse, and number of offspring. Of these 289, 4.8 percent went to neighboring islands, mostly to marry; 28.0 percent to the mainland (permanently rather than to prepare for emigration from Ireland); 42.8 percent to the United States; 22.8 percent to England; 1.0 percent to Australia; and 0.6 percent to Canada and other countries. The shift of emigration from the United States to England after the Second World War is revealed by the following statistics: between 1891 and 1945, 72.4 percent of Inis Beag emigrants went to the United States and only 10.6 percent to England; but between 1946 and 1958, emigration to the United States dropped to 25.5 percent, while to England it increased to 45.1 percent. The fact that before 1946 approximately 16 percent of the islanders who emigrated remained in Ireland as compared to 28 percent after that date attests to the increasing property in their homeland as well as abroad.

It is beyond the scope of this work to follow Inis Beag emigrants of the past and present to their destinations abroad and beyond; the causes, conditions, and consequences of emigration from Ireland to America and England are amply documented in such standard works as Cecil Woodham-Smith's *The Great Hunger*, George W. Potter's *To the Golden Door*, William V. Shannon's *The American Irish*, Arnold Schrier's *Ireland and the American Emigration*, and John A. Jackson's *The Irish in Britain*. But, in closing chapter and book, I would like to discuss two additional sets of statistics which have an important bearing on Inis Beag culture and personality and which, as far as I know, have never been compiled systematically for any body of emigrants from a particular locality of Ireland. One set deals with the place of origin and the religion of men and women whom islanders marry outside of Ireland, and the other concerns the frequency of marriage among those who have left the country.

Emigrants from Inis Beag have settled, for the most part, in Irish ethnic communities—near relatives—in large cities and their environs of the United States, England, Australia, and Canada. In the United States, these are greater Boston, Hartford, greater New York, Chicago, Milwaukee, and Oakland. The majority of them have had their transportation overseas paid for by relatives who emigrated before them and in whose communities they have made their new homes, and the first order of business for the newcomers is to repay the loans made to them for the journey. Of the first generation arrivals, 37.4 percent of them did not marry; of the remainder, 10.7 percent married fellow Inis Beag emigrants, 14.3 percent persons from Inis Thiar and other nearby islands, 40 percent Irish from the mainland, 8.9 percent Irish-Americans of the second generation and beyond, and 9.5 percent non-Irish. The unknown category is 16.6 percent and includes emigrants who no longer are in contact with their families in Inis Beag or who have married Protestants. As to the former, it is common for men to sever relations with their kinsmen at home when their mothers die, and even some daughters do so after they have been abroad a few years, especially those who have married non-Catholics or "foreigners." This reflects the Oedipus complex and religious and ethnic biases in the Inis Beag family, and runs counter to the assumption of nativists, primitivists, and functionalists who stress the strength of family ties in Ireland. The folk claim that no emigrant in human memory has married a Protestant, but I learned from islanders who had settled for many years in American communities of at least six who had done so.

Not only are the folk secretive about those of their number who have married Protestants after emigrating, but also about emigrants who have "lost the faith." By and large, these are young people who have emigrated to England since 1946; it seems that youthful emigrants before that time remained loyal Catholics, as have those who have gone to the United States recently. The widespread disaffection of Irish Catholics in Britain frequently is discussed in Inis Beag, and is blamed on the anonymity and "temptations" provided by the city. The "priest and gossip keep us faithful here" were the words of a man concerned about the rumored disaffection of his son in London.

During my last visit to Inis Beag in 1965, I discussed with over a dozen islanders some of the statistics that I had compiled previously and have reported herein. Without telling them the results of my analysis, I asked them whether more folk remained single in Inis Beag or abroad, and without exception they made the first choice. Their collective opinion is summed up by the remark of one that, "Here the old people interfere. They don't want to give up the land, and they don't want a new girl to come in. In America, the kids make up their own minds." Social scientists long have assumed that when emigrants from Ireland settle elsewhere, they soon come to marry as early and frequently as the people among whom they live, mostly because of changing economic conditions. But a single rate of 37.4 percent abroad, as compared to 28.6 percent in Inis Beag, belies both common and scientific sense. Certainly factors more important than economic ones are at work. Inadequate statistics for second and third generation Inis Beag emigrants suggest that the celibacy rate lowers markedly only when second generation, and beyond, descendants of emigrants disassociate themselves from Irish ethnic communities and Irish priests. Ethnographic research is sorely needed among Irish of several generations in the countries to which they have emigrated to probe this and other phenomena.

References

ARDREY, R., 1961, *African Genesis.* New York: Atheneum Publishers.

ARENSBERG, C. M., 1937, *The Irish Countryman.* Gloucester, Mass.: Peter Smith.

ARENSBERG, C. M. and S. T. KIMBALL, 1940, *Family and Community in Ireland.* Cambridge, Mass.: Harvard University Press.

BAUMAN, R., 1963, "John Millington Synge and Irish Folklore," *Southern Folklore Quarterly,* Vol. 27, pp. 267–279.

BECKETT, J. C., 1966, *The Making of Modern Ireland 1603–1923.* New York: Alfred A. Knopf.

BLANSHARD, P., 1954, *The Irish and Catholic Power.* London: Derek Verschoyle.

CAMPBELL, J. J., 1955, *Legends of Ireland.* London: B. T. Batsford, Ltd.

COXHEAD, E., 1961, *Lady Gregory.* London: Macmillan & Co., Ltd.

CURTIN, J., 1956, *Irish Folk-Tales.* Dublin: The Talbot Press Limited.

CURTIS, E., 1950, *A History of Ireland.* London: Methuen & Co., Ltd.

DELARGY, J. H., 1945, *The Gaelic Story-Teller.* London: Geoffrey Cumberlege.

———, 1957, "Folklore," *A View of Ireland,* J. Meenan and D. A. Webb, eds., Dublin: Hely's Limited, pp. 178–187.

DILLON, M., 1957, "The Irish Language," *A View of Ireland,* J. Meenan and D. A. Webb, eds., Dublin: Hely's Limited, pp. 207–220.

DORSON, R. M., 1966, "Foreword," *Folktales of Ireland,* S. O'Sullivan, ed., Chicago: The University of Chicago Press, pp. v–xxxii.

EVANS, E. E., 1957, *Irish Folk Ways.* London: Routledge & Kegan Paul, Ltd.

FREEMAN, T. W., 1960, *Ireland: A General and Regional Geography.* London: Methuen & Co., Ltd.

HARRIS, R. L., 1954, "Social Relations and Attitudes in a N. Irish Rural Area— Ballygawley." u.m.

HUMPHREYS, A. J., 1965, "The Family in Ireland," *Comparative Family Systems,* M. F. Nimkoff, ed., Boston: Houghton Mifflin Company, pp. 232–258.

INGLIS, B., 1965, *The Story of Ireland.* London: Faber & Faber, Ltd.

JACKSON, J. A., 1963, *The Irish in Britain.* Cleveland: The Press of Western Reserve University.

LEWIS, O., 1960, *Tepoztlan: Village in Mexico.* New York: Holt, Rinehart and Winston, Inc.

LEYTON, E., 1966, "Conscious Models and Dispute Regulations in an Ulster Village," *Man,* Vol. 1, No. 4, pp. 534–542.

MACNEILL, M., 1962, *The Festival of Lughnasa.* London: Oxford University Press.

MESSENGER, J. C., 1959, "Religious Acculturation among the Anang Ibibio," *Continuity and Change in African Cultures,* W. R. Bascom and M. J. Herskovits, eds., Chicago: The University of Chicago Press, pp. 279–299.

———, 1962, "A Critical Reexamination of the Concept of Spirits: With Special Reference to Traditional Irish Folklore and Contemporary Irish Folk Culture," *American Anthropologist,* Vol. 64, No. 2, pp. 367–373.

———, 1967, "The 'Black Irish' of Montserrat," *Eire-Ireland,* Vol. 2, No. 1, pp. 27–40.

———, 1968, "Types and Causes of Disputes in an Irish Community," *Eire-Ireland,* Vol. 3, No. 3, pp. 27–37.

O'FAOLAIN, E., 1954, *Irish Sagas and Folk-Tales.* London: Oxford University Press.

O'FAOLAIN, S., 1956, *The Irish: A Character Study*. New York: The Devin-Adair Company.

O'KEEFFE, J. G. and A. O'BRIEN, 1912, *A Handbook of Irish Dances*. Dublin: M. H. Gill & Son, Ltd.

OPLER, M. K. and J. L. SINGER, 1956, "Ethnic Differences in Behavior and Psychopathology: Italian and Irish," *The International Journal of Social Psychiatry*, Vol. 2, No. 1, pp. 11–23.

O SUILLEABHAIN, S., 1957, "The Feast of St. Martin in Ireland," *Studies in Folklore*, E. Richmond, ed., Bloomington: Indiana University Press, pp. 252–261.

————, 1963, *A Handbook of Irish Folklore*. Hatboro, Pa.: Folklore Associates, Inc.

————, 1967, *Irish Wake Amusements*. Cork: The Mercier Press.

O'SULLIVAN, D., 1961, *Irish Folk Music and Song*. Dublin: At the Sign of the Three Candles.

O'SULLIVAN, S., ed., 1966, *Folktales of Ireland*. Chicago: The University of Chicago Press.

POTTER, G. W., 1960, *To the Golden Door*. Boston: Little, Brown and Company.

SCHRIER, A., 1958, *Ireland and the American Emigration*. Minneapolis: University of Minnesota Press.

SHANNON, W. V., 1963, *The American Irish*. New York: The Macmillan Company.

TRACY, HONOR, 1953, *Mind You I've Said Nothing*. London: Methuen & Co., Ltd.

————, 1956, *The Straight and Narrow Path*. New York: Vintage Books.

WOODHAM-SMITH, C., 1962, *The Great Hunger*. London: Hamish Hamilton.

YEATS, W. B., ed., ND, *Irish Folk Stories and Fairy Tales*. New York: Grosset & Dunlap.

Recommended Reading

DANAHER, K., 1962, *In Ireland Long Ago.* Cork: The Mercier Press.
    The author is a member of the Irish Folklore Commission, and presents in this book a series of 26 short essays on facets of traditional Irish folk culture, with special emphasis on the economic aspect and material culture. Six of the closing chapters deal with balladry, factionalism, marriage, and the wake and funeral.
————, 1966, *Irish Country People.* Cork: The Mercier Press.
    This volume, a companion to the other, is a collection of 20 more vignettes. Of particular interest to my readers are "Tall Ships," "The Currach Men," and "The People of the Sea." Danaher's two books are literary as well as folkloristic works, and suffer only from the telescoping of historical epochs, a nonfunctional approach (common to folklorists), and occasional nativism and primitivism.

EVANS, E. E., 1942, *Irish Heritage.* Dundalk: W. Tempest, Dundalgan Press.
    The two volumes of the author (The other, *Irish Folk Ways,* is listed in References.), like those of Danaher, focus on the economic aspect and material culture, and are illustrated profusely with drawings and photographs of scientific import. Evans is a geographer-folklorist-anthropologist at The Queen's University of Belfast—the only university in Ireland which includes ethnology in its curriculum. My readers will be interested especially in the last six chapters of *Irish Heritage* and the last four of the author's other work, which take up such subjects as wrack, boats and fishing, festivals, weddings and wakes, and non-Christian religious forms (termed beliefs and superstitions by folklorists). Throughout both books are numerous references to the many island communities of Ireland.

FLOWER, R., 1944, *The Western Island.* Oxford: Clarendon Press.
    This is an account of the author's experiences during holiday visits over 20 years to the Great Blasket Island off the Dingle Peninsula of Co. Kerry. Flower was an English scholar, spoke Irish, and composed the book from lectures delivered on Irish literature at the Lowell Institute of Boston in 1935. It is a literary tour de force and a source of ethnographic data, if the intense primitivism of the author is duly weighed.

HUMPHREYS, A. J., 1966, *New Dubliners.* New York: Fordham University Press.
    Fr. Humphreys is a sociologist at Loyola University of Los Angeles, who studied peasant and Dublin families between 1949 and 1951. Although this volume deals mostly with family and class in Dublin, its first, third, and last chapters contain much material on Irish folk culture. The author addresses both the strong Oedipus complex in the family and puritanical Catholicism and their impact; however, he alludes to Augustinianism rather than Jansenism as the doctrine which inclines the Irish countryman "to a jaundiced view of sex" who "places a high premium upon continence, penance and ... abstemiousness" (pp. 23–27).

MASON, T. H., 1967, *The Islands of Ireland.* Cork: The Mercier Press.
    First published in 1936, this classic now in paperback reissue presents descriptive, historical, archeological, zoological, and some ethnographic data on a dozen of the inhabited islands off Ireland—including Tory, Achill, Clare, and the Blasket and Aran Islands. The author was a famous photographer, particularly of birds and wildlife, and an expert on Irish antiquities, while a Dublin optician.

MEENAN, J. and D. A. WEBB, eds., 1957, *A View of Ireland.* Dublin: Hely's Limited.
    Twenty-one essays, written by eminent Irish natural and social scientists and subsumed under 12 chapters, make up this volume published for The British

Association for the Advancement of Science. Chapters on archeology (by S. P. O Riordain and Francoise Henry), local traditions, and the Irish Language (by Myles Dillon) contain important articles on folklore (by James H. Delargy), place-names (by M. A. O'Brien), and folk life (by T. A. Lucas).

MULLEN, P., 1934, *Man of Aran*. London: Faber & Faber, Ltd.

Robert Flaherty filmed his famous documentary, *Man of Aran*, during 1932 and 1933, and the author served as his assistant. A native of Inis Mor, the largest of the three Aran Islands, Mullen wrote this book as an autobiographical account of his (and his neighbors') involvement in the filming venture. It is rich in dialogue, which many islanders feel best of all literary works captures their syncretistic English. The author now lives in Wales.

————, 1936, *Hero Breed*. London: Faber & Faber, Ltd.

The setting of this novel once again is Inis Mor, and the author sets down the most prominent features of the Aran way of life. Both of Mullen's works betray the exaggerations of pride and primitivism and neglect dysfunction, but this one best serves the self-image of the people, as many hold, although it is criticized locally for revealing pagan retentions. The author also published, in 1940, *Irish Tales* (London: Faber & Faber, Ltd.)—a collection of folktales that he had heard as a youth.

NEWMAN, J., ed., 1964, *The Limerick Rural Survey*. Tipperary: Muintir na Tire Rural Publications.

This book includes five lengthy reports (the last by Fr. Newman) by Irish scholars, based on research done in Co. Limerick between 1958 and 1964 under the guidance of American and Dutch social scientists. It represents the first full scale study of the "developmental infra-structure of an Irish county." Its strength for my readers are the 15 chapters which make up the reports on demography and social structure (by Patrick McNabb), while its main weakness is a disregard for religious and psychological variables in accounting for certain phenomena.

O'BRIEN, J. A., ed., 1954, *The Vanishing Irish*. New York: McGraw-Hill Book Company, Inc.

The causes of "the fading away of the once great and populous nation of Ireland" (p. 3) are examined in this collection of 19 chapters written by 16 authors (Fr. O'Brien has four.). Jansenism and sexual puritanism are dealt with most effectively in chapters by Bryan MacMahon, Sean O'Faolain, Arland Ussher, and two by the editor. These themes and their consequences also are discussed in the polemical, but deeply insightful, *The Irish and Catholic Power*, by Paul Blanshard —listed in References.

O CROHAN, T., 1951, *The Islandman*. Oxford: Clarendon Press.

Complementing Flower's book on the Great Blasket Island are three written by islanders themselves, which are autobiographical in nature and of value to students of Irish folk culture: O Crohan's and those by O'Sullivan and Sayers. O Crohan's volume was published first in Gaelic in 1929, then translated into English by Flower in 1937—"the first attempt by a peasant of the old school . . . uneducated in the modern sense, though . . . trained in the tradition of an old folk culture, to set out the way of his life upon this remote island from childhood to old age (p. v).

O FLAHERTY, T., 1934, *Aranmen All*. Dublin: At the Sign of the Three Candles.

Like Mullen, the author was a native of Inis Mor and was stimulated by the film, *Man of Aran,* to write his two works dealing with the milieu there. The book is magnificently illustrated with stills from the movie and photographs taken by Mason. Part anecdotal and part imaginative in composition, it rivals Mullen's volumes in providing ethnographic materials.

————, 1935, *Cliffmen of the West*. London: Sands & Co.

Both of O Flaherty's books present sketches—some of them printed previously as newspaper features—of various segments of the Aran tradition at the turn of the century. They contain much folk English dialogue, as do Mullen's volumes, but are far less primitivistic in orientation than the latter. All writings of Blasket and Aran islanders emphasize ideal rather than real culture.

O'SULLIVAN, M., 1957, *Twenty Years A-Growing*. London: Oxford University Press.
Four years after O Crohan's book was published, this work appeared in both Irish and English, and in 1935 was revised by its translators, Moya Llewelyn Davies and George Thomson. It is a series of vignettes, as *Aranmen All,* rather than a life history, as *The Islandman,* which ends when the author as a young adult leaves his home to become a policeman on the mainland, where he died in 1950.

SAYERS, P., 1962, *An Old Woman's Reflections*. London: Oxford University Press.
The author, who married into the Great Blasket Island from a community on the nearby coast, was a famous *scéalaí*—rare among women—known as "the Queen of Gaelic story-tellers" (p. ix). In this volume, translated from Irish by Seamus Ennis, she recounts anecdotes from her colorful life. Writers and critics argue among themselves as to the relative literary merits of this work and those by other unschooled islanders of Ireland; but most agree that O Crohan's has no peer, an opinion with which I tend to agree. As to depth of insight into Irish folk culture and personality, however, I would choose *Twenty Years A-Growing.* To the ethnographer, the chief value of Sayers' book is that it presents a "woman's-eye view" of things Irish.

SYNGE, J. M., 1966, "The Aran Islands," *J. M. Synge Collected Works*, Vol. 2, A. Price, ed., London: Oxford University Press, pp. 45–184.
John M. Synge, most famous as a playwright, spent five months during summers from 1898 to 1902 in the Aran Islands. Out of his experiences there came *Riders to the Sea* and plots of other plays, as well as this chronicle of the local culture of Inis Meain—the middle Aran isle—published in 1907. Although an exceptional work of art, it suffers from primitivism, a lack of concern for the importance of Catholicism in the lives of the folk, and the projection of the author's tragic view of life into his interpretations. An excellent appraisal of Synge as a folklorist is found in Bauman 1963.

CASE STUDIES IN CULTURAL

ANTHROPOLOGY

GENERAL EDITORS — George and Louise Spindler

HOLT, RINEHART AND WINSTON, INC.
383 Madison Avenue, New York 10017